5 Steps to a Happy, Healthy, Wealthy YOU!

through music, the mind and meditation

Benjamin D. Koen, Ph.D.

SOUND HEALTH
GLOBAL

5 Steps to a Happy, Healthy, Wealthy YOU!
through music, the mind and meditation

by Benjamin D. Koen, Ph.D.
Copyright © 2014, Revised Edition © 2018 by Benjamin D. Koen

Published by **Sound Health Global,** www.soundhealthglobal.com
and also available through:
www.happyhealthywealthy.me
www.benkoen.com
www.amazon.com/author/health

ISBN-13: 978-1-941977-01-9

The Benefits of Dr. Ben's Meditation Program

When you meditate and connect with the power of your soul,

all things are possible.

Your body grows in strength and vitality.

Your mind becomes clear, focused, and peaceful.

Your spirit becomes free and powerful.

Your emotions become positive, joyful, and enthusiastic.

Your relationships become healthy and beautiful.

Your wealth and prosperity increase.

You add value to the lives of others and bring light to the world.

True Happiness, Health, and Wealth
lie within you.
They are your birthright, and unfold with
each moment of meditation.

DEDICATION

All my thanks to you, my readers, students, friends,
clients and colleagues, who have used the material
in this book to breakthrough any limitation and
create the lives you desire.
Thank you for sharing your successes,
struggles, triumphs, and transformations with me.
I am honored to work with you.

Contents

First, a few thoughts

... heart to heart

In your hands is an offering from my heart to yours. My intention is that the spirit and energy of this book will connect with that place deep in your heart and soul where you are fully aware that you are a beautiful, wondrous, eternal, and joyful being. From that place of wholeness and oneness within you, that place where all is well, you will learn clear and practical steps on how to extend the energy of your soul (vital force) throughout your body, mind, emotions, relationships, and life in order to create all that you can imagine.

This book stems from more than thirty years of music making and meditation, as well as over a decade of research and applied practice, all of which have helped me to overcome my personal challenges and become a happy, healthy, wealthy, and spiritual being, full of love, strength, energy, peace, and enthusiasm. The powers of music and meditation continually transform my life and I see them transform the lives of others daily, in ways both great and small.

If you truly desire to create happiness, health, and wealth in your life, this book is for you. You don't need to know anything about music or meditation to benefit from this book. It is not about making music or being a musician, but rather about how the powers of music and meditation can work together to help you create the life you dream of. This book is a sharing of what I know to be a powerful way of wellness and healing, a way of transformation, a way of happiness, a way of wealth, and a way of manifestation.

Along with my personal experience of knowing and living through the powers of music and meditation, my research into these powers has explored how and why music, specialized sound, and meditation can help you to create the life you desire. I have come to believe and know that you can create health and healing, a clear, focused, and peaceful mind, empowered and joyful emotions, unified and vibrant relationships, wealth and prosperity, and the spiritual qualities that fill your heart and life with love, laughter, vitality, serenity, and strength. I have shared the principles and practices in these pages with hundreds of people spanning a broad diversity of backgrounds, who without fail when they practice these simple yet powerful techniques, are able to transform their thoughts to a higher state of consciousness, achieving and often far exceeding their personal goals.

Through the myriad concerns of daily life, attention to the past, and worry about the future, you may have forgotten who and what you truly are, what you are capable of creating, and how beautiful life can be. This book is a way to return to your true self—a self that is pure, beautiful, knowing, loving, strong, giving, peaceful, and able to create anything you desire. By immersing your thoughts in that subtle and generative state of meditation where all potentials exist, you become aware of your true self and strengthen the connection to the source of your being. Then, by learning how to extend that energy into your daily actions, you can manifest the reality that your soul inspires. Briefly put, this book will enable you to enliven your connection to your inner spirit and let that energy flow into all aspects of your life, creating a sea change in the invisible quality and manifest reality of your existence.

The ideas, skills, and practices that you will learn here focus on music and meditation as ladders for the ascent of your soul, the transformation of your life, and the manifestation of all the potentialities of your heart. When you climb these ladders daily, you will experience positive change and even transformation in every aspect of life. Most importantly, remember to have fun! This is a practice and a process, not a one-time event. So, enjoy every moment of the beautiful journey you are about to begin!

How To Use This Book

The sweet fruit of meditation is mindful action.
The sweet fruit of mindful action is personal and world
transformation.

~

XIAMEN ISLAND, CHINA, 10 A.M. FRIDAY

She was all smiles, full of enthusiasm, with just a smidge of disbelief. This is how one of my top doctoral students entered class that day. She had just finished reading a section of my first book and she was ready for an easy route to fat loss.

She sat down and looked at me, excitedly. "You mean that if I meditate, I can lose weight? I'm ready! Tell me how."

Everyone is ready when there is an easy way that requires no personal action—you know, the get-rich-quick approach to life. Of course, she was thinking that there was a magic fat-loss meditation to which I held the secret. Without missing a beat, I smiled and said, "Absolutely you can, if you have the right meditation! First, tell me what is meditation to you?" She had not yet taken any of my seminars on meditation, so this was a new conversation for us. She went on to describe it as a basic idea of clearing her head, deep breathing, and finding a peaceful state of mind ... and that was it. Well, that can be fine for some things, a quick relaxation response to de-stress in the moment, if you will. It can even be used to create more peace in life overall, if practiced regularly. But it was certainly not going to help her achieve the body and energy she was looking for. Neither will that approach help you reach your dreams or create the life of happiness, health, and wealth that you desire.

The reason is because her approach to meditation was not aimed at any focused action and had no specific goal for the post-meditation part of life—i.e., the rest of her day, every day, after meditating. I explained that naturally there are many different kinds of meditation, and that most have a special approach, technique, purpose, goal, or outcome. They are fine for some things and not for others. If you want to change and improve your body, heal yourself, or create a specific outcome and reality in your life, this book will help you do it.

"The kind of meditation you will need to achieve your goal to redesign your body is what I call my SEA Meditation," I said, "which stands for See, Experience, Act."

SEA Meditation Outline

See, Experience, Act

1. *See* the end in the beginning
   (See your end goal clearly at the beginning of any endeavor)
2. *Experience* that end as real, now, in your meditation
3. *Act* as though your goal has already been achieved

The SEA approach lies at the heart of the 5 Steps to a Happy, Healthy, Wealthy YOU!

This is one of the central themes that will be repeated and shown in different ways throughout this book. It is a key which, when practiced consistently, can be used to open the door to your new life full of all that you have imagined in your heart and mind. Use this book as a guide. You can modify practices to best suite your situation, but follow the principles and processes, which will provide a sure way to create a Happy, Healthy, Wealthy You!

This book will walk you step by step through these five steps. Let's take a quick glance at them now.

5 Steps Outline

STEP I: REFLECT

You will reflect on the Five Factors of life (body, mind, spirit, emotions, relationships) and write down where you are now and what you passionately desire to create in each of these Five Factors, and in life as a whole.

STEP 2: DECIDE

You will then choose which is the most important—that which you simply must have or be—from among all the things that you have written in Step 1.

STEP 3: PREPARE

You will take a moment to prepare your body to meditate. (This can take from a few seconds to a several minutes).

STEP 4: MEDITATE

You will enter the state of meditation and see that which you have chosen as being fully real and true now in your meditation. You will become that which you have chosen in your meditation. You will feel the sensation in your body, heart, and soul that you are that reality, and that reality is you.

STEP 5: ACT

You will arise from your meditation and immediately take action in your new reality.

Brief Background and Purpose

This book builds upon four broad areas of knowledge: Science, Spirituality, Music, and Experience. I have used the material in this book in research projects and with clients in one-to-one and group settings to help them achieve their life goals. I also draw upon my work in Medical Ethnomusicology which is a new and innovative area of integrative and holistic research, applied practice, and performance at the intersections of music, health science, HICAM (holistic, integrative, complementary, and alternative medicine), indigenous and traditional music and healing practices, neuroscience, the healing arts, spirituality, quantum physics, psychology, and anthropology. In addition, this book is also deeply informed by my experiences in nearly fifty countries with culturally diverse practices of music, prayer, meditation, health, and healing, as well as eternal spiritual principles that are shared among traditions across the globe. Lastly, I draw from my lifework as a musician dedicated to bringing forth music as a ladder for the soul, higher consciousness, happiness, health, and wellness—in brief, to create oneness, wholeness and freedom.

My purpose here is to share what I have learned and what I practice to create happiness, health, and wealth in my own life. Although it is true that any given program will not work for all people, I am happy, indeed thrilled, to be able to say that everyone I know who has used this program has achieved or far exceeded their personal goals in one or more areas of life. I am deeply honored to share this with you now.

CHAPTER 1

You Are Soul

*Sooner or later, you discover that
you are the master gardener of your soul,
the director of your life.*
–adapted from James Allen

Meditative Mind and Bridging the Gap

Have you ever tried to change your thoughts to create the
life you long for, but have been overwhelmed by countless
conflicting thoughts racing in every direction? Have you
tried to reach your dreams but become discouraged because
they aren't quickly realized? If so, you are not alone. So many
people struggle to try and create the life they desire in their
heart of hearts, but fail for one simple reason. They have left
out the most essential step: Meditation—the practice of
making conscious contact with your inner spirit, higher
consciousness, or your soul—YOU. From that beautiful and
powerful dimension of the soul, which is your personal

connection to the source of all being, all things are possible. Now, a quick point about the word "soul". By soul, I want to express the dynamic, unlimited and creative you—the generative you—the you that can generate and create whatever you become aware of and stay aware of. This is the you that has no limits and can also be called your inner being, higher consciousness or awareness, and which is part of what we can call the universal consciousness. Ok, now let's look at the relationship among your thoughts, mind, consciousness and meditation.

In one sense, it is true that You are what you think—but there is more to it, MUCH MORE! You are more than what you think. The maxim As you think, so shall you be takes you closer to understanding the power of thought and the role that the mind plays in transforming your life in any area that you desire—but for the vast majority of people, there remains a gap between the fact that your thoughts create your reality and to change your reality, just change your thoughts. This book closes the gap and opens the way to a new life through sound, music, and meditation.

Many people try to bridge this gap through positive thinking and have limited success at best. Certainly, positive thinking is important, but to achieve lasting change, to transform or heal your life, or to create anything that you desire, you must meditate. Meditation creates a new and wonderful mind, filling every moment with thankfulness, joy, and a deep sense of knowing, which leads to a different category of thinking beyond positive thinking—an empowered type of thought I call spiritual cognition, which emerges from your meditative mind and is an expression of your soul.

In other words, through meditation, you can transform the very fabric of your mind to the point where negative thoughts simply cannot emerge from it since there will not be anything negative in it to begin with. Consider that you can only get out of something what is already inside of it. For example, you cannot get orange juice from a coconut. In the same way, you cannot get negative thoughts or actions from a positive and spiritualized mind. The 5 Steps is a holistic approach to health, happiness, wealth, and manifesting your best life. The concepts and practices that you learn here build upon experience and knowledge that you already have, but may not have yet recognized that you possess. First, however, we must start with a new understanding about the transformative powers that music and meditation inherently possess, something I call the five powers of music, meditation, wellness, and wealth.

Five Powers of Music, Meditation, Wellness, and Wealth

Music and meditation are two of the greatest gifts you have to experience the transforming power of your soul. The five powers that music inherently possesses are the same powers that we find in meditation, health, and healing. These five powers are also the same as the five dimensions that comprise a human being, and which, when developed, lead to happiness, wellness, and wealth. I call these five powers and dimensions the Five Factors, since they must be actively factored into your life to create a new, healthy, and vibrant reality: they are the physical, psychological, emotional, social, and spiritual factors of life, also known here as the body-mind-spirit-emotions-relationship connection.

The Five Factors are explained in detail below. I introduce them here to highlight the underlying dynamic that causes you to listen to music, a dynamic that is linked to, and can transform, your body, mind, relationships, emotions, and spirit.

Why We Need Music

Why do we instinctively turn to music or specialized sound to create a desired emotion or state of change? Put simply, music is the language of the soul—it is the language of your inner, eternal, true self. Music is also food for the soul. Therefore, the soul seeks expression through music and sound, and is also nourished through music and sound. When you instinctively turn to music, it is the spiritual action of your soul that manifests your desire to listen to or experience music—it is the soul's need for expression or nourishment that compels you to express and experience yourself through music and sound—usually by listening, singing, making music, or dancing, as well as by sharing your favorite music with friends face to face and through social media.

Like music, meditation and prayer are also the language of and food for the soul. Here, we now see a great relationship among music, meditation, and prayer beginning to emerge. While there are multiple aspects to these relationships, what is most important to highlight now is that music and meditation are often interrelated, and at times are one and the same.

At their heart, music and meditation are ladders for the soul that connects us to our spiritual reality. Equally important is that music is a vehicle of meaning and energy— that is, every song, sound, or piece of music carries and gives meaning and energy to the listener. That meaning and energy then effects a change in the listener. I'm sure you've had the experience when hearing a song or piece of music that makes you recall a memory from a long time ago and you are flooded by those same emotions you felt at that time in the past; or where you use music to give yourself incredible physical energy to accomplish some goal—maybe when working out, exercising, running, winning at some sport, getting motivated to achieve a goal at work or school, or simply to relax.

You've probably also used music to create a special environment to achieve other goals, like setting the mood for a romantic encounter, building energy in a group for a meeting or event, calming down the energy of an individual or group of people, helping yourself sleep or wake up, to intentionally remember a particular time in your life or experience specific emotions, to forget something or someone, to escape a particular situation or memory, or to feel better, stronger, happier, or healthier. I'm certain that you've already used music to change your state at a specific time for a specific reason and you already know that music can change the feeling and experience of your body, mind, emotions, spirit, and relationships.

Music and meditation can balance, integrate, and recalibrate your entire being. In fact, music itself is a kind of meditation. Music is a ladder that is expressed through the interplay of sound and silence. So, since music is both a language of the soul and food for the soul, we can say that we need both sound and silence to be whole and healthy. The soul is wholly and without exception good, beautiful, knowing, true, and worthy. Music strengthens your soul and increases its presence in your life. The soul is always seeking to ascend to greater heights of spirituality; music lifts the soul up and gives it power. While music has Five Factors, I must emphasize that music's essence is spiritual—just like your essence, you are soul.

From this vantage point, read the following three lines, then pause, breathing naturally and deeply, and allow the essence of meaning to permeate your being:

Music strengthens and empowers my soul.
When my soul is strong and fully present in my life,
all is well and I can achieve anything.

How Can I Think about Meditation?

You can think about meditation as one of the essential nutrients for your soul, mind, body, emotions, and relationships. Meditation is also a process, which, over time, progressively transforms your mind into one that is wholly positive by nature and therefore can only produce positive outcomes.

For a moment, consider your mind to be a garden that is populated by all kinds of beautiful plants and flowers, each one representing a wonderful and positive thought. However, the garden that is your mind can also spawn weeds, which represent negative and self-defeating thoughts. Meditation does not focus on pulling the weeds; rather, meditation simply does not give attention to the negative thoughts. This is tantamount to not providing water and sunlight to the weeds, causing them to eventually fade away and die. Meditation gives full attention to that which is positive and good, spiritual and true, giving light, food, and water to the flowers and plants of your mind (your positive thoughts) so they will grow, multiply, and bear the fruits of a happy, healthy, and wealthy life.

Spiritual thought is creative and generative by nature—that is, once enlivened, spiritual thought naturally creates and generates that which is within it. Think of this as a seed that is planted in fertile soil and receives sunlight and water—it will bear the fruit that is potential within it. The wonderful and empowering reality about this dynamic is that YOU decide what seed to plant in the fertile soil of your consciousness.

Through your new meditative mind and spiritual thought, a fresh reality will naturally emerge that is reflective of your new consciousness. Consider that your life at this very moment is an exact representation of your present state of consciousness, which is a function of the degree that your soul is the prime mover in your life, and which depends on the quality of the attention of your mind.

As you learn to immerse your attention in the dimension of your soul, you will gradually release all manner of limited thinking, your heart and mind will expand and be recreated, and your life will reflect and manifest all the spiritual attributes that are latent within you. Through the power of music and meditation, the fabric of your consciousness is transformed and automatically brings forth the reality that your soul inspires.

In addition to the limited positive thinking approach for creating a new life, many people try to meditate, but become frustrated because they don't experience any special state of consciousness, or they don't see or feel tangible results immediately. So, they try another form of meditation, and then another, without success—like someone who wants to lose weight who jumps from one diet plan to another, and then another, and another, finally giving up and concluding that either they have a genetic problem and they can't lose weight, or that they are simply meant to be overweight. Similarly, people having difficulty with meditation might conclude that it just doesn't work for them. If you have had this frustrating experience, it is likely that meditation was presented to you as a complicated, esoteric, or dogmatic practice that either forced a particular form onto you or privileged one person or tradition over another, creating a façade of spiritual hierarchy and dependency by telling you that you need a master or guru, further distancing you from true meditation, which is one of the most vital and natural practices in which you will ever engage.

Meditation is as natural as breathing—having both universal and very individual aspects. Once you taste the sweet and gentle power of consistent meditation, which will transform your life in myriad ways, both great and small, you will come to see that meditation is as essential to life as water, food, air, sleep, shelter, love, and light. You will long to return to your sacred space of meditation on a daily basis every morning and evening. As you develop an intimate and conscious relationship with your soul, you will soar further into the blissful heights of a spiritualized consciousness, savoring every step and every breath of life as a precious gift, extending the spiritual power of your meditative mind throughout the world, and bringing forth a fuller expression of the oneness of the spiritual-physical reality.

Sounds Good—Now What about Money and Wealth?

Wealth is a belief, an emotion, an experience of love, of giving and receiving; it is a mindset and a knowing that you are an abundant being, right now, as you are, regardless of how much money is in your bank account, or how high your net worth is.

There are plenty of financially rich people in the world who aren't wealthy! Sure, wealth can include being financially rich, but true wealth is not dependent on money. Before we get into some details, let's consider a few thoughts about wealth:

It is health that is real wealth and not pieces of gold and silver.
–Mahatma Gandhi

All the breaks you need in life wait within your imagination. Imagination is the workshop of your mind, capable of turning mind energy into accomplishment and wealth.
–Napoleon Hill

Wealth, like happiness, is never attained when sought after directly. It comes as a by-product of providing a useful service.
–Henry Ford

Health is the greatest gift, contentment the greatest wealth.
–Buddha

Whoever does not regard what he has as most ample wealth is unhappy, though he be master of the world.
–Epictetus

No amount of money can ever make you wealthy.
–Tony Robbins

All riches have their origin in mind. Wealth is in ideas— not money.
–Robert Collier

When you know what true wealth is, then and only then are you ready to be financially rich.

~

So, you might be asking, "OK, so if this is wealth, then what is financial freedom?" In the beginning, most people think that financial freedom means being a millionaire, or living a lifestyle of the rich and famous, or maybe just "being rich." But what do these ideas really mean? And, better yet, what specifically does it mean for you to be financially free?

When people stop to genuinely think about what it would mean for them to be financially free, they realize that the dollar amount is actually far lower than they originally thought it would be. Also, they usually see two stages as precursors to financial freedom. The first is financial security, where all your debts are covered and where your investments generate enough cash flow to provide for all your basic necessities of life. The second is financial independence, where you are debt free, you never have to work again, and where, in addition to your necessities being provided for, basic life entertainment, travel, and some other extras that you desire are also covered. After that comes financial freedom, where you are debt free, you never have to work again, and the cash flow generated from your investments is enough to cover everything that you can imagine you might want.

One measure in the last two stages is that you never have to work. However, for a fulfilling life, you will work because your work is something that you love to do, as it adds value to your life and to the lives of others.

Five Realizations about Money and Wealth

Five of the most important realizations you can make about the financial and material part of life are:

1. Material wealth, prosperity, and abundance are far more than just money; they are a state of mind and emotion, an experience, a consciousness, a way of being.

2. Material wealth, the ability to create money, prosperity, and abundance are within you and you can manifest them in your life when you add value to the lives of others.

3. Material wealth, money, prosperity, and abundance are a result of your beliefs, thoughts, and actions being rightly directed.

4. Your beliefs, thoughts, and actions being rightly directed includes more than focusing on money and business; they must also encompass your body, mind, emotions, relationships, and spirit.
5. You must have a financial plan with clear, effective strategies and take consistent measurable actions toward your financial goals.

This book gives you a holistic approach to life transformation and creating the total life you desire. From this perspective, and in the experience of people who have already gone through the process, true wealth is experienced as one progressively does the practices beginning in chapter 9 (but, remember, don't skip ahead; you must read the whole book, from start to finish, in order to achieve the greatest success). Building from this, financial freedom becomes a by-product of the practices. The focus is on the foundation out of which true wealth and financial freedom arise. I cannot overemphasize how important this foundation is—and that the foundation is you! True and enduring wealth and financial freedom can only be built on a strong and whole foundation.

Today, there are so many resources available on investing and the mechanics of how to make your money work for you, whether you have no idea where to start from, or if you are more experienced with money, or if you are a sophisticated investor; whether you like the stock market, real estate, companies, business, commodities, or a combination of these. If you don't have the wealth and financial freedom you desire, most likely the mechanics aren't the problem. All that you will have in the future with respect to your wealth and money will emerge from you, so YOU are the most important factor for your wealth and financial freedom. This book focuses on YOU—all of you, so that the foundation from which your wealth arises will be strong and capable of creating and sustaining true wealth and financial freedom.

Universal Principles and Processes

A key to making meditation successful is to understand a bit about the universal principles and processes that underlie and inform diverse practices of meditation. By learning about these principles and processes, and actively applying them through the steps presented, you will not only be equipped with the knowledge and skills to successfully meditate, but you will also have begun a lifelong process of unfolding wondrous and amazing aspects of yourself that lie just beneath the surface of your daily awareness. Through the power of music, the mind, and meditation, you will access the level of consciousness that is pregnant with the life you desire, and which longs to be born into your daily awareness and manifest in your every thought.

Your soul self is always quietly whispering to you beneath the noise of a frenetic mind, attempting to guide you in every moment, in every circumstance, in every decision, and in every action. The more you connect to that level of your soul consciousness, the more that guiding voice will emerge into your daily awareness, the more the noise of senseless concerns will fade away, and the more your daily actions will embody the truth and beauty of your spiritual and creative energy.

Even if you think that you cannot meditate, this book shows you that you already have and that you are quite good at it! Building upon your inherent capacities and experiences, this book sets out a course that is flexible enough for everyone to use—and it works because you are a co-creator of your practice! You will learn how to achieve your goals and get lasting results in the areas of your body, mind, spirit, emotions, and relationships, all of which will facilitate the flow of happiness, wellness, and wealth into your life.

CHAPTER 2

Your Internal Super Powers

*The most common way people give up their power
is by thinking they don't have any.*
–Alice Walker

*Wake up, seize the day, live now to the fullest;
there is nothing else, and this is bliss.*

~

Manifesting Your True Life

Within you there exist very real super powers that comprise a dynamic and one hundred percent effective system that always succeeds at achieving its goals. I call this your

Internal Super Power Success System (or SUPER POWER SYSTEM for short).

Although you have had this fail-proof system your entire life, and although it functions flawlessly 24 hours a day, 7 days a week, 365 days a year, you are likely not fully aware of it. When you understand what these powers are and how they work, they will enable you to move from being a passive observer sitting in the passenger seat of life to sitting in the driver's seat of the life that only you can imagine, that you deeply desire and decide to manifest.

Your Super Power System naturally follows, supports, and even rallies around the focus of your attention, taking you closer to realizing that which occupies your thoughts. With every synapse that fires within the neural networks of your brain, a link is made in a chain of events that takes you step by step toward manifesting your thoughts into reality, thereby creating success.

The only catch is that this system will naturally move toward succeeding at any goal, even one that is not good for you.

This system is like the engine of a car—once it is turned on, it will go wherever the driver focuses her or his attention and decides to go. For example, if you drive your car the wrong way down a one-way street, the engine will not intervene and say, "Excuse me, but you have decided to go the wrong way. But don't worry—I will correct your mistake. Go this way." Even if you have a talking GPS mapping system in your car that verbally tells you, "You're going the wrong way—turn around," it cannot turn the engine off;

neither can it change your course. On the contrary, the engine will continue to take you forward until you change your mind and act or until you crash. In this way, the engine is totally disengaged from what is right or wrong, or what is best for you—it simply provides the energy for motion. Your Internal Super Power Success System works the same way.

Whatever you turn your attention to, your Super Power System will immediately respond, and begin to carry you toward that goal, just like the engine. So, if you decide to focus your attention on service to others, adding value to people's lives, love, happiness, wealth, strength, or compassion, your Super Power System will respond just as it would were you to focus your attention on obstacles, problems, why things don't work, anger, frustration, or stress. Fortunately, if you learn to meditate and link into your soul, creating an unbreakable bond with your spiritual reality, your Super Power System will naturally and immediately be oriented toward that which is good, beautiful, and creates prosperity, happiness, and wellness. In brief, through meditation, you can have a super-powered system to achieve anything you set your meditative mind to. Let's explore the components of this system in more detail.

Components and Functions of Your Internal Super Power Success System

The Power of Neuroplasticity

You are probably wondering: So how does it work? What is this Super Power System that is inherent in me, that is custom-made to help me attain my deepest goals? First, I should say that this system is composed of what can be considered capacities, principles, and processes that propel us toward that which we focus our minds on. By learning a bit about these components, you will better understand the process of transformation and the power of your thought in the process.

The first component or power of your Super Power System is neuroplasticity, the brain's natural capacity to transform itself through experience and interaction in the world, including all manner of action, thought, attention, and meditation. The discovery of neuroplasticity is revolutionizing the way we understand the power of the human brain and the world that we create from our minds.

The long-standing notion of the brain being a fixed, hardwired organ that is inflexible is slowly melting away. One of the most interesting things that we are learning in the cognitive and neurosciences is that much of our understanding about the power of the brain is directly related to our beliefs about the brain's capacity, as well as the degree to which we practice that which we want to create. A key aspect of creating a new mind and life is the capacity of cognitive flexibility—a kind of openness and flexibility of mind (discussed below), which nurtures neuroplasticity.

Briefly put, neuroplasticity is the brain's way of solving any functional problem it confronts. For example, if the neural pathways for moving the index finger of the right hand are damaged or destroyed, the brain can solve this problem by generating other neural pathways to perform the same function, or by allowing existing pathways to take over the task. In addition, neuroplasticity is simply a general operating principle of a healthy brain, actively building new neural pathways wherever they are needed.

A key point here is that you have neural patterns in your brain right now that are, in part, directing the course of your life, and underlying all the emotions and experiences that you are presently having. What the dynamic of neuroplasticity tells us is that, no matter how deeply embedded and hardwired those neural pathways seem to be, no matter how rigid and unchangeable you might think they are, they are not—they can and do change according to what you think and do, and YOU have the power to decide exactly what to think and do.

For example, in biological research, scientist Anna Gilsen was able to teach Swedish children a skill that was previously thought to be possessed only by children of the Moken sea nomads, who live in the area of the Indian Ocean that was tragically hit by the tsunami of December 26, 2004. The Moken children are famous for being excellent deep-sea divers. Underwater, one's vision becomes blurry since light is refracted through the water and cannot interact with the retina in the same way as when one is above the water. Over time, the Moken children have developed a specialized ability to constrict their pupils some twenty-two percent by changing the shape of the lenses in their eyes. As young children, they did not try to change the shape of their lenses; this just naturally developed as a capacity from doing or practicing the right thing—in their case, deep-sea diving over and over again.

Controlling the lens and size of the pupil was previously thought to be a natural reflex that was hardwired in the brain and nervous system and could not be changed. So, when Gilsen taught Swedish children to do the same thing as the Moken, the only response had to be for researchers to expand their minds with respect to human potential—specifically that the flexibility, neuroplasticity, or changeability of the brain is possible. Your thought patterns and their underlying neural architecture are malleable and can be totally transformed.

What is even more wonderful than this discovery is how the capacity for change is not limited to the biological or the physical parts of life, but also relates to your emotions, thoughts, and behaviors. Now, you might not be interested in deep-sea diving, but you will be interested in diving into the sea of your consciousness and the ocean of your soul, where the pearls you find are priceless and not of this world. The way to plunge into this limitless sea of possibility is through the practice of meditation, which can totally transform you.

Simple and profound, meditation works in multiple dynamic ways, with feedback loops between all parts of the Five Factors of your being. In part, through neuroplasticity, meditation creates new patterns of neural activity that bring forth the emotions and experiences that you want to have and the life you want to manifest. However, the central way that meditation can bring about transformations is through the dynamics of experiencing your higher consciousness and soul during the high point of your meditative practice. A key connection to extending the power of meditation into your daily life is in the next component of your Super Power System, Cognitive Flexibility.

The Power of Cognitive Flexibility—the Open Mind

A closely related core capacity that is essential for transformation is the power of cognitive flexibility. This can also be called thought flexibility or more commonly as having an open and active mind. In my work, cognitive flexibility has a twofold meaning: it refers to your inherent ability to transform from a lower state of being to a higher state, emphasizing the role that your conscious thought plays in this process; and it also refers to a state of consciousness that is a bridge between the lower and higher states. The lower state is often called the lower self, lower consciousness, or ego—it is a dimension often characterized by negative thoughts and emotions, obstacle seeking, stress, worry, depression, illness, or disease. The higher state is often called the higher self, higher consciousness, or spiritual self—it is a spiritual state that is categorically distinct, since it is defined by an absence of all things negative or degenerative, of stress, depression, illness, and disease; and it is expressive only of positive and spiritual qualities, of peace, health, vital energy, joy, certitude, and wholeness. The dynamic in-between state of cognitive flexibility is a steppingstone between the lower self and the higher self; the lower consciousness and the higher consciousness; the limited self and the limitless self; the physical self and the spiritual self.

The powerful role that cognitive flexibility plays in restructuring the self cannot be overly emphasized.

Cognitive flexibility is a bridge to a transformative type of mystical experience that is naturally oriented toward wholeness and oneness. It is also a process by which you let go of the lower self and surrender to your higher nature; it is a progression whereby you move from divisive, negative, or dualistic thinking into the blissful state of oneness. The state of oneness that you will enter at the height of your meditations is a core experience of pure consciousness, which automatically integrates spirit into your being and brings a healing energy and deep sense of happiness and thankfulness to you. When you consider that all aspects of a human being are interrelated, you can see the inherent power of cognitive flexibility as the transformational influence of thought within your being at any given time.

The most important point here is that music naturally engenders cognitive flexibility. Just ask yourself what happens to you when you listen to music that you love. Your mind, emotions, body, and spirit immediately change, moving in fresh and positive ways. A lighthearted and effective example I often use in my seminars and workshops to show how music immediately changes our state of being through cognitive flexibility is the tune "My Girl," performed by the Temptations. I start to play the recording, but after the first three notes of the tune (played on the electric bass), I stop the recording and virtually every face in the audience is smiling and a clear emotional shift has already occurred. Then, usually people call out for me to keep playing the recording—that is, not to withhold the rest of the wonderful emotional experience they know they will have by listening to that song. So, I begin again from the top. This time I let a few more notes play so people go a bit further into the song, building their expectation of experiencing all the emotions and physical sensations they associate with that song. But then I stop the song again and the audience gasps and calls out once more, "Play the song! Play it! Don't stop!" So, I oblige—but just before the vocal track comes in that says, "I've got sunshine on a cloudy day," I stop the recording one last time. As though on cue, the crowd yells out loudly for me to keep playing the tune, and although they are a bit bothered, they all have smiles and are laughing because they get the point of the example—namely, that all their lives they have been using music as a tool of cognitive flexibility and to create a desired state of being.

Now, the only thing to do is to use that newly created state of consciousness to plant the seed of a generative idea in your mind that will grow into the new reality that you desire for yourself. It slowly becomes clear that music can be used exclusively as a meditation practice, as a way to experience the cognitive flexible state, or as a way to develop the skills of cognitive flexibility, which can then be utilized even without music. The key, however, is to not stop there, but rather to understand the purpose of that specialized state of consciousness. The purpose of cognitive flexibility is to allow us to move into our higher selves and incorporate more of that spiritualized state into our whole being and daily experience. The next component of your Super Power System is known as entrainment and is a key factor in doing just that.

The Power of Entrainment

You might be wondering: "How is it that, from this state of cognitive flexibility, I can naturally move toward a spiritual state where I can experience all that is good—total health, joy, and bliss?" In other words, you might be asking yourself: "If I can get into this flexible state of consciousness, why should I naturally move only into a state of higher consciousness—a soul-state of awareness? Why couldn't I drift into a lower state?" The answer to this and related questions is found in one of the physical laws of nature and its counterpart in the spiritual dimension of life.

This law is known as entrainment, which is the synchronization and unification of two separate vibrations (oscillations, frequencies, or rhythmic processes). Dutch physicist Christiaan Huygens first documented the phenomenon of entrainment in the mid-1600s. He placed two pendulum clocks in close physical proximity and discovered that, although at first the clocks were out of sync, they soon began to synchronize and unify their movement—they entrained. Some theorists say that entrainment is nature's way of conserving energy. My strong sense, however, is that entrainment is nature's desire for unity, which then creates an increase in power or energy. In the process of entrainment, the weaker rhythm gives way to the stronger rhythm. For Huygens, the clock with the stronger pulse entrained the weaker one. It can also be seen that rhythms of similar strength will move to a middle ground as they entrain to each other. The key point is that entrainment, like gravity, is one of the physical laws of the natural world, which simply operates when the right conditions are present.   I   n physical entrainment, the essential condition is close physical proximity. So, if two clocks are placed far apart, they will not entrain, but when they are close enough, they will entrain—they will become unified and be as one. The same dynamic is true of in the biological realm. For example, if a newborn has a weak or irregular heartbeat, when that baby is placed close to a newborn with a strong and regular heartbeat, the weak heart will slowly entrain to the strong one and become healthy.

Building upon this dynamic in the context of meditation, rather than a close physical proximity, a close proximity of your consciousness to your soul is needed—I call this spiritual entrainment. Now, since the soul is non-material, transcendent to the physical world, and, by definition, timeless and placeless, you might ask: How can I get close to it? This is where the power of music, the mind, and meditation is key. Music, the power of your mind's attention, and meditation are conduits to the mystical dimensions of the soul. Through them, you gain skill and experience in developing a spiritual closeness and subsequent connection to your soul. And, when this closeness and connection is made, it transforms everything—the body, mind, emotions, relationships, finances, business, work—everything.

When your mind gets "close" to your soul, then the process of spiritual entrainment will naturally and automatically occur. As your meditation deepens and you move through the process and state of cognitive flexibility, you can gently let go of any psychological or emotional attachments you have and surrender your present state of consciousness to your higher consciousness—your personal will surrenders to the will of the greater good, and your lower self entrains and becomes one with your higher self. If we relate this dynamic to the clock example, we can say that the soul has a stronger power of attraction, a stronger energy than the mind; however, if the mind stays far away, it will not entrain with the soul. If, however, you bring your mind close to your soul, it will give in to its spiritual reality and the source of its being—it will spiritually entrain with your soul. Then, your mind becomes transformed instantaneously, miraculously, and without forceful effort.

Since this kind of experience evokes a deep sense of beauty and bliss, and can change your life in positive ways that seem almost unbelievable, I should emphasize the importance of being fully in the moment and keeping in mind that meditation is a daily and ongoing process, not a one-time event. This point is key to creating sustained and complete transformation. Consider that what often happens after a powerful experience of meditation is that many people, understandably, get swept up in the event of meditation, thinking that they have achieved enlightenment, and then they become disappointed when that wonderful feeling gradually drifts away. They then think that such an experience was a fluke, not real, or that they have failed in their attempts to become truly enlightened. Unfortunately, such discouragement is often enough to send a person back to their old ways and rut of life—forgetting about meditation and the importance of staying in conscious contact with the soul.

What you must remember is that meditation is not a one-time event, no matter how profound one meditation session might be. Rather, such an event must be seen as one step in a larger process, and as a window into the limitless state of enlightenment, a state that is independent of, and transcendent to, the material world, but which is also related to bringing about an enlightened and unified world. Moreover, even if one can surrender the ego and become enlightened, there are always higher stages that one can reach within the never-ending dimensions of enlightenment. In the next chapter, you will be introduced to the last two components of your Super Power System, which you will see to be of great assistance in creating enlightenment, happiness, health, and wealth in your life.

Keep in mind, just as spiritual entrainment occurs when you bring the focus of your attention into close proximity with your soul, the opposite can also occur—if your attention gradually drifts away from your soul and closer to an ego-centered life, the lower self gains control and the power of your soul fades into the background. So, a key goal is to extend the precious and powerful experience of meditation into the rest of your daily life and to sustain it. You will achieve this through a daily practice of meditation every morning and evening, linking the events or practice of meditation into the journey of life. Your life then becomes a never-ending form of meditation and not only transforms your life, but also contributes to the spiritualization of the planet.

CHAPTER 3

Every Morning and Evening

Meditate every morning and evening,
then see your new life unfold before your eyes.
~

You Are a Great Monk!

A story I learned while studying and teaching the health and healing practices of *qi gong* and *tai ji* in the northeast of China is apropos here. The story tells of a great spiritual teacher who was advising his students, all of whom were on a disciplined path of learning to become monks. The students had one year left in their training and great interest in their future life once they achieved enlightenment, which was to happen around the end of their training. All the students thought that during their last year of training they would complete all the disciplines of a monk's life and continue to live in the mountains far away from the worldly pursuits and concerns of their fellow citizens. The students thought they would lead a simple life, pray and meditate, live in peace, and only tend to spiritual matters. "After all," they thought to themselves, "we are monks and that is what monks do."

One morning after breakfast, the students asked their teacher, "If you have been training monks for years, why are there no other older monks here in the mountains with us? There are only you and us. Where are all the monks that you trained that we have heard so many incredible stories about? Where do they live?" The wise and loving teacher smiled and drank the last drop of tea in his cup. "Gather all your belongings," he said. "We are going on a journey." For three days, the teacher led the students down the great mountain, walking in silence, and at times singing a gentle melody that blended perfectly with the sounds of nature around them.

As they approached the foothills, the teacher and students stopped and gazed at the bustling, almost chaotic markets below, where countless of people were busily going about all the activities of daily life. With the solitude and peace of the mountains now behind them, the students were not sure why they had come to look at the people, but they were confident that they would soon return to the peace of their mountain home and their teacher would explain it to them. But, instead, the teacher continued down the last stretch of land before the market. The students followed. As they approached the market, they could see people of all ages and backgrounds: a few were happy, but most were not; most were in pain or suffering. The teacher stopped once again, and turned to face his students. He looked up to the mountain that reached into the sky behind them and said, "I will now answer your question about where all the monks are that I've trained. But first you should know that there are two kinds of monks, those who live in the mountains and those who live in the market. The ones in the mountains are good monks, but the ones who live in the market are great monks! The reason why there are no other monks in the mountains with us is that I only train great monks, and the only way to become great is through actively serving and educating humanity, not by just praying and meditating, but through action. Now, you are all ready to do great things, to live among the people, serving, bringing enlightenment to the world, not just to yourselves. Your last year of training begins now, living with the people in the market and villages. And remember: peace, power, knowledge, joy, and healing are within you—you are the mountain, you are the reflection of the rays of sunlight, you are the flowing stream of the great river that leads to the ocean of light, you are the leaf that gently floats in the wind above the treetops. The beauty and power you recognize in our mountain home is just a reflection of your own hearts. Open your hearts to the world and know that *you are soul.*"

The students remained silent for several minutes as they contemplated what their future would hold. One student then asked, "Master, may we never return to see you at the top of our mountain home, in that beautiful place we've grown to love?" The wise and loving teacher answered, "Dear ones, you must return, every morn and eve, I will be waiting for you." Another student asked, "How is this possible, Master, when the journey takes three days?" The teacher gently closed his eyes, inhaled a pure and deep breath, exhaled, slowly opened his eyes, and said, "The only way to ascend the mountain every morn and eve is through meditation. In that sacred space of your enlightened mind, where we are all one, you can ascend that spiritual mountain that is not made of rock and dust, but of light and love. This is the true mountain that has no physical peak. There, among the windflowers and streams of light, will we meet as one soul. There, will you refresh and rejuvenate your spirit. Then, as you arise from meditation, will you carry that loving energy to all beings great and small."

There is more to the story, but the key point of action is clear—you must act to fully embody the benefits and blessings of meditation and to create true growth and lasting transformation. That is to say, as you take action in a spirit of service to your fellow human beings and as you add value to others' lives, blessings and spiritual power will be given to you and emerge from you. This is a truth that you will also experience when you take but one step in the path of meditation and spiritualizing your life.

The transformation is a process of focusing your mind and attention on that which you desire to be and incorporate into your life, internalizing and manifesting it. This process forms the next power in your Super Power System that I call embeingment, which means to fully internalize something in your whole being, not only your body.

Attention – Internalization – Manifestation

The Power of Embeingment

When you meditate and arise to extend the experience of your higher consciousness into the rest of life and share that light with the world, you not only incorporate and internalize that energy into your body (embodiment), but also into your entire being—including your mind, emotions, spirit, and relationships. I like to call this holistic embodiment, or embeingment, since it more accurately describes the dimensions of a human being that is transformed through music and meditation—that is, through meditation, you can incorporate whatever you desire into your entire being, not just your body.

Embeingment then, is the next dynamic component of your Super Power System that is a process of **attending – internalizing – manifesting**. That is, as you turn your attention to and become aware of your soul, you will progressively internalize the spiritual effects experienced through this conscious contact. Then, you will naturally manifest into the fullness of life what has been internalized. This new state of being brings forth a fresh and spiritualized quality of attention, which gives momentum to the cycle repeating itself, each time with progressively higher quality and purer frequencies of vibration experienced in your being and manifested in your life. It can be seen as an upward spiral, progressively becoming broader, encompassing more virtues and serving to more effectively add value to people's lives (see Figure 1). With each expanding and spiraling cycle of attention – internalization – manifestation, you will incorporate more of your soul into yourself, manifesting your higher consciousness, happiness, health, and wealth in all aspects of your being and life. With each cycle, you move from strength to strength, growing stronger, happier, wiser, more thankful, humbler, and more spiritual.

Upward Expanding Spiral of Embeingment
Higher Consciousness – Happiness
Health – Prosperity

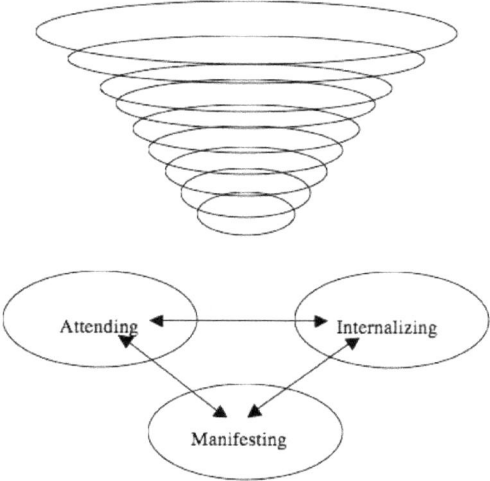

Figure 1: Attending – Internalizing – Manifesting

Donna's Dilemma

Let's look at an example from one of my clients. Donna is a young adult who desperately wanted and needed to lose weight. Her obesity not only affected all aspects of her self-identity, emotions, and relationships, but she was also at the early stages of developing diabetes at age nineteen, which would worsen her already depressed state, lead her into another cycle of illness, and potentially lead to heart disease, stroke, and even death.

Like so many others, Donna tried numerous diets but was never able to make any significant or lasting change in her weight. The only outcome of her attempts was a growing frustration, depression, and sense of failure. If we look at what her thoughts were, it becomes clear that she was actually very successful at manifesting the thoughts she had in her mind—the only dilemma was that the thoughts in her mind were overwhelmingly negative: thoughts of illness, depression, self-hatred, disgust, anger, loneliness, stress, sadness, and being "fat." As she directed the power of her repeated ATTENTION to those negative qualities and states of being, she INTERNALIZED them and continued to MANIFEST them in her life.

It is important to note that her state of illness did not come overnight, from one negative thought—quite the opposite. Her state was a result of years of repetition and conditioning herself to a response. So, from this perspective, she was already an expert at manifesting the life she had in her mind. The only thing she needed to do was change what was in her mind. In other words, she needed to change or spiritualize her attention to what her soul-self desired, rather than what others desired for her or what she believed she was supposed to desire. If she could create a mind that reflected and focused ATTENTION on the joy, health, love, and prosperity of her inner being, this would naturally change what she would INTERNALIZE and MANIFEST.

Once she started the 5-Step program of music and meditation, which began with an in-depth reflection and concise self-assessment, she was able to progressively expand her understanding of her body and her being, framing them in a greater reality that gave her the power to change anything about herself. For example, before learning about and practicing meditation, Donna had a limited view of her body and embodiment—that is, losing weight was merely a physical task that would subsequently be manifest only in her body. This is not to say that she never thought of the other aspects of her being. She did. The dilemma was that she viewed losing weight as a solely physical task. So, Donna focused on the physical—eating or not eating food, taking diet pills, and exercising, always negatively comparing her body to the images she saw in magazines, the media, and countless young women lost in a storm of materialism. Moreover, she had little understanding of the nutritional and energetic value of the food she was eating, she did not understand the physical, psychological, and emotional side effects of the diet pills she was taking, and she almost never had enough energy and motivation to exercise, in part because of the pills and type of food she was consuming, but also because of her previous bad experiences with exercise.

The reason that her previous attempts to lose weight failed was that her goal and motivation were not only negatively formed, but they were also solely focused on her body and totally detached from the rest of her being: her mind, emotions, relationships, and spirit. Nevertheless, her FAILURE to lose weight should actually be seen as the SUCCESS of her Super Power System, which led her to the FAILURE she had in her mind!

Gradually, through the music-meditation program, Donna's mind became open and flexible, allowing fresh, positive, and health-giving qualities to be the focus of her attention. She then shifted her goal and approach in a few key ways, which eventually brought about the beautiful life she subsequently conceived in her mind.

Donna's New and Wonderful Mind

First, Donna replaced the goal of losing weight with the goal of being healthy. There are a few empowering concepts in this initial shift. First, being healthy emphasizes an ongoing state of being that is positive, empowering, success-oriented, and sustainable, whereas losing weight is negative, limited, and impossible to sustain, since losing weight is almost always viewed as a one-time event or hopelessly unsustainable over a long period of time. Second, being healthy speaks to all Five Factors of Donna's being—her body, mind, emotions, relationships, and spirit—whereas losing weight was narrowly viewed as only pertaining to one of the Five Factors, her body. Third, in addition to the new goal being cast in positive terms, it further describes and encourages a way of living, specifically being healthy, which, as I discuss further in chapter 4, engenders cognitive flexibility through an empowered phrase or cognitive link. The cognitive link of being healthy serves as a bridge between her higher state of consciousness during meditation and her experience outside of meditation throughout the day.

Cognitive links serve as a way to pass the tests in life that are necessary for growth, and, in one sense, this was the crux of the matter for Donna, since each test had the potential to create either feelings of confidence and strength if she passed them, or doubt, disappointment, and depression if she failed. So, developing the skill and power to make good decisions and take the subsequent healthy actions was key.

Let's look at a specific example: Donna was challenged to maintain the presence of her higher self through the tests of the day, specifically to be healthy when she had to make decisions about what to do, eat, feel, or think. Here, the power of the cognitive link can be seen in the immediacy of its effect. For instance, after Donna would meditate effectively in the morning, the reality of being healthy was strong. Subsequently, when she was confronted with what to eat for breakfast, the self-identity of being healthy was tested by a host of food choices, some of which were healthy and others that were clearly not. Since she had just made being healthy the focus of her meditation, there was a fresh and strong cognitive link that was very present in her consciousness and allowed her to choose something healthy, even if she had a competing cognitive association with an unhealthy food that she happened to like.

The reason that the being-healthy cognitive link could topple the link associated with the unhealthy food is that, when Donna experienced the thought of being healthy, her brain immediately enlivened the neural network that was created and strengthened during the highpoint of her meditation, which was a true experience of herself as being healthy, strong, and beautiful. As we will explore in more detail below, when you experience your higher consciousness in meditation, it is not an abstract vision or a weak imagined experience; it is a real experience that carries the power to transform your life. Hence, for Donna, the being-healthy cognitive link released a whole body and whole being response that brought the power of her higher self from meditation to manifestation at the very moment she had to make a decision about what to eat. The result was that being healthy outweighed the desire to eat a food that was unhealthy. This was not just important in the physical factor of life for Donna, but in all the other factors as well, giving her confidence and the experience of success, control, empowerment, courage, and a sense of self-worth that she experienced in not just her body, but also her mind, heart, and soul, and which then made a categorical difference in her social experience throughout the day.

Another important result for Donna was that, after a week of consistent meditation, it occurred to her that she faced the same test about what to eat every morning. So, she decided to clean out her refrigerator and throw out all the food that was unhealthy. She did this based on a simple whole-foods approach we had researched together. Basically, she threw out all processed foods, anything with partially hydrogenated oils, high-fructose corn syrup, artificial sweeteners, or artificial colors. After that, there wasn't much left in her refrigerator! She then went shopping for some whole foods and had a wonderful experience. Once she did this, not only did her sense of personal power increase, but she also created a healthier living environment in which to start her day.

The beauty of strengthening this approach is that being healthy is positive knowledge that creates a positive space of consciousness where negative knowledge has no power to exist. It is exactly like the relationship between light and darkness. Darkness has no independent existence of its own; it only exists when there is an absence of light. In other words, darkness is dependent on the absence of light. Light is a positive energy that is independent. Darkness can only exist where the positive energy of light does not exist. In the same way, when you have positive knowledge, a positive consciousness, or positive psychology in the deepest sense of the term, there is no room for negative thoughts to enter. Truly, the only way that a negative or dark thought can exist is in the absence of a positive or enlightened mind, which literally is a mind full of light.

Now, consider Donna's experience when she was living with the old goal of losing weight. In the morning, she would often pray to God to help her lose weight, and even hope for and think about losing weight, but she never had the power to make healthy choices regarding food. Why? There are two reasons.

First, on the one hand, there were gaps in Donna's thinking and brain activity between the existing neural networks that were focused on the goal of losing weight and her ability to actually lose the weight and be healthy on the other hand. As I came to know Donna and guide her through the assessment process and meditation practice, it became clear that, although losing weight was labeled as her original goal, it was couched in a host of negative associations, like failure, lack of power, low self-esteem, and disappointment, and it was further supported by years of life experience of making repeated unhealthy choices. So, from the perspective of the broad landscape of her mind's attention, she was focused on or attentive to a complex of negative behaviors, which she then succeeded in attaining. In other words, Donna focused her attention on that which was unhealthy, and she attained and maintained that goal of being unhealthy. Moreover, she had spent many years practicing negative thinking and behaviors, which in essence habituated her to a negative outcome. She had become an expert at creating negative outcomes.

Second, the negative cognitive links associated with losing weight brought forth immediate negative responses in the moment of decision-making. In this way, in the critical moment of making a choice about what to eat for breakfast, in the flash of a moment, she would experience a host of emotions that created a state of already having failed. So, she naturally followed that state of mind, later felt depressed that she did not have the strength to eat something healthy, and yet at some level accepted this, since it was supported by her internal negative goals and state of mind.

Let's return now to why the holistic understanding of embeingment is important in the process of transformation.

In Donna's case, her initial approach to losing weight was a limited view of the body as being only physical and disconnected from the rest of who she was as an intellectual, emotional, social, and spiritual being. Simply put, she viewed herself primarily as a body that needed to lose weight, and all her associations about that process were negative. Once she expanded her understanding of herself through the meditation program's assessment process and gained a little experience about the connections among her body, mind, emotions, relationships, and spiritual faculties, she knew that any transformation she wanted to create in her body must be accompanied by an equal transformation in her mind. Furthermore, she learned that any lasting change in her mind cannot come through positive thinking alone, or a disconnected type of struggling to reach a goal that was ultimately negative. Rather, she learned that she must link her mind to the great power of her soul, from which emerged such goals and realizations as being healthy, vital, energetic, strong, and beautiful. Through this experiential process, all her doubt slowly faded away, replaced by a certainty of her true reality. This CERTAINTY is something that every human has. It is a quality of knowing that you possess in your heart of hearts, in your innermost being, and it is the final component of your Super Power System.

The Power of the Human Certainty Principle

This component of your Super Power System is what I call the Human Certainty Principle (HCP). This is a deep knowing beyond intuition, belief, and faith that emerges in stages as you practice meditation. Notably, the HCP is related to the well-known Heisenberg Uncertainty Principle (HUP), which describes the uncertainty inherent in measuring two parameters of a particle at the same time, for example, position and velocity. This is related to what is called the observer effect: that the very act of observing a controlled experimental environment can change that environment. In a similar way, we constantly influence the quality and content of our lives through the power and quality of our attention. Through meditation, you can transform the power and quality of your attention to create the life you desire—specifically by experiencing your higher consciousness and extending that spirit into all aspects of life.

When you enter the transcendent state of your higher consciousness in meditation, you move from the physical world of the uncertain into a spiritual state of certitude or certainty, a state that is knowing, peaceful, and humble. In this state, any uncertainty that is manifest in the workings of the physical world or your life experience is sensed as being part of the greater spiritual reality and purpose for your life. This sense of certitude engenders confidence, courage, gratitude, calmness, wisdom, and joy, and it represents a mind shift from fear, stress, and anxiety to an absence of fear and doubt, and the experience of peace, lightness of being, steadfastness, and strength.

In summary, the components of your Super Power System are intimately linked to the Five Factors of music, meditation, health, and your ability to manifest the focus of your attention. Before moving to the next section, read aloud the following lines, breathing naturally and deeply as you read and relax into the meaning of the words, and allow your whole being to internalize their truth:

I can choose my thoughts.
My thoughts lead to my actions.
My actions create my reality.

I choose to center my thoughts and my attention on my soul and all the spiritual attributes that are within me—love, unity, peace, forgiveness, compassion, detachment, strength, courage, certitude, flexibility, openness, wisdom, health, wellness, wealth, joy, and happiness.

I am thankful that I have the power to act on my thoughts and to create the life that I imagine.

I am thankful for my Super Power System, which naturally takes me closer to what I think about and where I direct my attention.

I now command my subconscious mind and my Super Power System to achieve all that is best for me and in harmony with the greater good.

CHAPTER 4

What is Meditation, Really?

See into your heart and know all truth.

~

Knowing Your True Self

To meditate literally means to focus your mind, clear your mind, or to be in a special state of mind or being. But ask yourself: "Who is focusing my mind through meditation?" Or "Who is clearing my mind through meditation?" The typical answer is "I am focusing or clearing my mind." But ask yourself "If, through meditation, I am focusing or clearing my mind, who is this 'I' that is observing and doing this with my mind?" In other words, WHO or WHAT AM I if I am more than my mind? What a wonderful question! Often, approaches to meditation stop at the first step of you observing your mind without asking the question Who is this observer? At times, people ask the question, but leave the answer in a vague and diffuse definition of consciousness.

The crux of the matter is to go beyond the stage of observing the mind and make conscious contact with the observer, which is your spiritual center, your soul, your true and eternal self, and then to surrender to your soul, allowing your soul-self to become your only self. Without this basis of experiencing your soul power and realizing that the soul is your true self, the transformational power of meditation is lost and it becomes a kind of band-aid, where the power of your attention is only given to the surface level of any situation rather than the core or root.

Carl's Core Condition

Let's consider the difference between dealing with an issue on the surface level vs. at its core, with respect to health and healing. For example, Carl had a skin condition whose root cause was a disruption in his life force that manifested itself through a series of psychosocial stressors from dysfunctional relationships.

Neither Carl nor his physician tried to find the root cause of the condition, content to treat it on the surface—literally on the skin—by simply applying a cortisone cream and other topical lotions, which at first seemed to heal the problem. But, after some time, when the stress of any relationships peaked, the condition reappeared, only this time in a more severe manifestation. Outdated thinking would view the skin condition as the problem, whereas new thinking views the skin condition as a symptom of a deeper problem or dis-ease. Rubbing cream on it is just treating the symptom, which might have a minimal effect on the surface, but can never heal the underlying problem, and can even have a detrimental effect by suppressing the symptom and causing it to go to a deeper energetic level of a person's being. Alternatively, treating the person's underlying state of being from which the skin condition arose creates the possibility of a cure. This occurs through a transformation of consciousness energy that permeates all aspects of a person's being.

Meditation is similar. It can function on the surface level and have a minimal effect, or it can be a bridge to your core being, your soul—a fountain of incredible energy that knows no bounds. Once contacted and more fully embodied, the soul naturally recalibrates your being: your body, mind, emotions, and understanding of your relationships. This soul energy is beyond the limitations of the physical world, because it is not composed of physical elements. Your soul, your true self, is a higher order of energy and creation than your physical body or the natural world. By nature, your soul is unlimited and capable of miraculous feats—it is healing, unifying, edifying, emboldening, light giving, peaceful, joyful, and perhaps most important, your soul is knowing. Your soul is your personal bridge to the reality of oneness. When you are living fully from the bridge of your soul, you embody all the potential of the universe and are a master of your life.

Meditation and Oneness

The core experience of participants in the studies I have conducted on music and meditation is the experience of oneness or unity within themselves, with all people, and all of creation. Most importantly, when participants have this experience, they feel a sense of oneness with all people, not just a narrow group of insiders defined by religious, cultural, ethnic, or any other labels. One of the most memorable occasions that illustrate this point occurred during and after a regular group meditation whose participants were very diverse. There were many world cultures and beliefs represented. What is striking is that there was a commonly shared experience among such a diverse group. As participants climbed the ladder of their musical meditation, they slowly ascended to a rarefied space of higher consciousness where they each experienced a connectedness, wholeness, and oneness with each other and all people that was not limited to any specific group.

One of the profoundly transforming results of repeatedly experiencing this dimension was that all participants found a deep sense of peace within themselves and subsequently experienced and created more peace in their own lives. In other words, the experience of oneness or unity facilitated peace within participants individually, as well as within their personal relationships and daily social interactions. Notably, while all participants experienced relaxation, calmness, and a decrease or elimination of stress early on in their meditations, they did not experience that categorically distinct emotion of peace until they experienced oneness via their soul selves.

It is interesting to note that the more you transform yourself, the more you benefit the entire planet. For instance, building from these and other experiences of the participants mentioned above, we can see that oneness or unity is a prerequisite to lasting peace for each individual, as well as for the whole of humanity. To me, this provides another great reason to meditate. Certainly we should endeavor to establish peace in the world in hand with nurturing a greater understanding of oneness, yet it is a key realization that true and lasting peace depends upon our collective recognition of our inherent oneness as a human family, which is a typical experience in deep meditation. Otherwise, social and global peace will not be built upon a firm and secure foundation, and will fall at the first test that challenges the unity of its participants. A cursory glance over the last century at attempts to create peace without oneness is sufficient to show the vital need for oneness in the world. When a true sense of oneness is established in the hearts of all the diverse peoples and countries of the world, peace will naturally emerge on the global stage as one of its fruits.

Experiencing Beauty and Truth

In the courses and workshops I give, even the most skeptical participants are transformed by experiencing the power of their meditative minds. Once they experience just a taste of that specialized state of being inside meditation, where there is no judgment, pain, failure, ugliness, doubt, hate, envy, or tiredness, and only unconditional love and acceptance, health, success, beauty, certitude, energy, and truth exist, participants have a transformational experience, which becomes a touchstone that they build upon through their successive meditations. Even if the first taste of that rarefied state of meditation lasts for just a moment or several seconds, that is enough to show that within you, at the core of your being, you are only beautiful and good, and that you possess a power that is creative in nature, and which, when directed toward your goals, will naturally create exactly what you introduce into that generative state of meditative consciousness.

Little by little, through your music and meditation practices, the inside state extends further and further, eventually becoming your outside state of being as well. That is, as you go through the 5 Steps, your outer life will reflect a progressively greater degree of the spiritual essence that is your soul until there is no more outside and inside because they merge to become one and the same, totally unified. This is when life becomes a meditation or prayer and one moves by the power of the spirit that is an ever-present and all-pervading essence, the uncreated, the beginning that has no beginning and the end that has no end. This is the state of being that is attributed to the enlightened souls that have inspired people throughout the ages to express their inherent nobility and beauty at all times, to focus on that which is good, and to manifest only beauty and goodness in the world. As the poet John Keats so eloquently wrote:

Beauty is truth, truth beauty,—that is all
Ye know on earth, and all ye need to know.

Keats's poem articulates a wonderful dynamic that is at the heart of meditation. Specifically, that when you reach a certain state of meditation and you are in contact with your soul, you overwhelmingly experience beauty, which is truth. Arising from meditation, you will have the profound sense that indeed, that is all you know on earth, and all you need to know. As you develop this knowing, your daily experience, your actions, responses, decisions, emotions, thoughts, and insights emerge from this knowing of beauty and truth, thus creating a life that is beautiful and true, in the deepest sense of the word.

CHAPTER 5

Unity and Conscious Contact

Where there is unity there is always victory.
–Publilius Syrus

Your thoughts create your reality. Use them wisely.
~

Conscious Contact and the True Self

What conscious contact means is that your true self, your soul, becomes the overwhelming presence in your life and you live and move from that place of being. Music and meditation help you to make conscious contact, creating a familiarity and stronger relationship between your daily self that exists outside of meditation and your soul-self that you come to know inside meditation.

The self inside meditation is categorically distinct from the self outside of meditation. The self outside of meditation is limited and uncertain; the self inside meditation is limitless and knowing. Consider the following chart (Figure 2), which was part of one of my research projects where participants were asked to describe themselves and their identity both inside and outside of meditation. To do this, they answered these questions:

1. Who am I and how do I see myself outside of meditation?

2. Who am I and how do I see myself inside of meditation?

3. In their responses, they gave both one-word or brief answers and longer answers that ranged from a paragraph to a few pages. Figure 2 is a chart of the most common one-word/brief answers.

WHO AM I?

OUTSIDE MEDITATION	INSIDE MEDITATION
Ugly	Beautiful
Sad	Joyful/Happy
Angry	Peaceful/Calm
Self-critical	Accepting
Hopeless	Hopeful/Knowing
Physical/Body	Spiritual/Beyond a body
Defined by others	Defined by true self
Worldly	Spiritual
Limited	Limitless
Fat	Healthy body
Stressed	Peace/Calm
Doubtful	Certain/Confident
Alone	Connected
Unloved	Loved
Unworthy	Worthy/Valuable
Insecure	Secure
Stuck/Immobile	Flying/Free
Unfocused/Chaotic	Focused/Organized/In control
Tired/Exhausted	Awake/Energetic
Addicted	Free
Abused	Healed/Whole
Victimized	In control
Shy	Confident
Weak	Strong
Sick	Well/Whole
Unhealthy	Healthy/Vital
Judgmental	Accepting/Understanding
Worried	Peaceful/Certitude
Fearful	Fearless
Incapable	All things are possible
Stupid	Knowing
Flawed	Perfect
Heavy in heart and mind	Lighthearted
Prideful	Humble
Disconnected	Oneness/United with all
Self-absorbed	Concerned with serving others
Egocentric	Egoless
Poor	Wealthy/Rich
Needy/Dependent	Generous/Independent

Figure 2: Outside/Inside Meditation Chart

Participants wrote much more than could be added to this list, but the point is clear—there is a stark difference between the states of consciousness when one is outside meditation and when one is inside meditation. Moreover, consider that through your thoughts, attention, and the actions they bring about, you start to believe and eventually become whatever you think about and focus on.

But what if a person has had the outside-of-meditation list as the fabric of their daily awareness and self-identity for five, ten, or even twenty or more years? Some of the people I work with at times have such a concern, saying, "I've seen myself this way for so many years. How can I change?" The encouraging and indeed wondrous thing about the power of music and meditation is that once a person makes a decision to embark on a path of meditation, a natural process begins that is not bound by time or space. No matter how long a person has lived with false notions of the self, or had negative experiences that arose from miseducation or another person's hurtful actions, meditation can transform this into a new reality. Through meditation, what previously seemed like an unchangeable aspect of personal identity becomes nothing more than a cloud in your thoughts that you allow to float by your mind's eye and exit your consciousness forever.

All participants in this project, once they were able to spend just a moment's time in meditation where they caught a glimpse of their true selves—selves that are aligned with the inside-of-meditation list—they experienced an excitement and empowerment that is impossible to fully describe in words. Participants often say it is like waking up for the first time and finally being truly alive; that the feeling is like the power and freedom one experiences while flying in a dream; and that they find an authentic experience of what they instinctively know to be their true selves deep within their hearts.

Conscious Contact and Other People

I then posed similar questions to the participants, but instead of asking them to say how they viewed themselves, I asked them to answer the following questions:

1. Who are **other people** and how do I see **other people** outside of meditation?
2. Who are **other people** and how do I see **other people** inside of meditation?
3. How do I view **life** and the **world** outside meditation?
4. How do I view **life** and the **world** inside meditation?

It was surprising to most participants that the answers to these questions were very similar and at times identical to their previous sets of answers. Overall, the way we view other people and life itself is a direct reflection of how we view ourselves, which is a direct reflection of the quality of our attention and the degree to which our thoughts express our inner spiritual reality. The most important point to highlight is the stark contrast between perspectives when someone is inside meditation vs. outside meditation—or living from the higher vs. lower self. From this vantage point, the benefits of meditation for yourself and the whole of humanity become clear. Through meditation, we become aware of truths of which we were previously unaware, we become fair-minded, nonjudgmental, and open to change; we seek to create goodness and beauty at all times; we develop wisdom and insight; and we become expressions of oneness, happiness, wellness, and wealth.

As you progress in your meditation, you will begin to notice low (or negative) energy, as well as high (or positive) energy in people, places, and things, including what you see in the media, what you read, the music you listen to, the people you interact with, and in your own mind and body. Overall, you will be more aware and perceptive.

You will also have the mindfulness to know when to avoid low-energy people, things, and food. As you grow, you will notice that, at times, low-energy thoughts from others can be transformed in your presence. But a word of caution here: as you grow in your meditation and your embodiment of higher spiritual energy, the ego is ever ready to sneak in and make you think that you are perhaps more special or gifted than another person—be very aware of these thoughts and immediately refocus your attention on the good in people. If you are unable to do this, then focus your attention on the source of all good, spiritual qualities, or something that makes you feel humble and happy. If this too is difficult, then there is a surefire way to nip negative or judgmental thoughts in the bud: that is to remember your own faults rather than the faults of others.

Again, you should not dwell on your own shortcomings; on the contrary, you should entirely forget them to the point that they never enter your mind. However, if the ego tries to enter your mind and take over, you should quickly put out that fire, even if the only shortcoming you can remember is that very moment of having negative thoughts about another person or having superior thoughts about yourself. Remember, your Super Power System will naturally and unfailingly carry you toward whatever you focus on, especially when the power of your emotions is connected to your thoughts. So, keep this power directed toward your higher being and that frequency of energy that soars above negative thoughts, and it will serve both you and the greater good.

Personal and Global Peace

Equally important is to recognize that the difference you create in your own life through meditation will also play a role in transforming the world from a lower state of being that is expressive of the outside-meditation list to a higher state of being that is expressive of the inside-meditation list. In other words, since our thoughts literally create a new reality, both positive and negative, we must keep them spiritually directed to bring forth a spiritualized and unified planet.

Planetary transformation and spiritualization moves at a rate that is often difficult to discern in the here and now, being hidden within the complex social conflicts that are the bitter fruit of de-spiritualized, exclusionary, materialistic, and non-meditative attention, thought patterns, and education. Simultaneously, the integrative and generative process of the confluence of a growing spiritual consciousness of countless people across the world increases the momentum of both the personal and global spiritualization that we are part of when we get in conscious contact with our soul self through meditation.

Through our personal and collective endeavors of manifesting all the spiritual attributes that are our birthright as humans, we begin to see that our transformative processes of meditation become laden with a power and import that is nothing short of making our lives and the world a reflection of a spiritual reality that is, by definition, fully alive and creative, exuberantly joyous and beautiful, an expression of balance and wholeness, a manifestation of oneness, and, at long last, at peace.

Climbing the Ladder of Music and Meditation

Common among all schools of meditation is the experience of transforming the quality, direction, openness, and power of your attention. Most often, people are in conscious contact with everything except their soul. You can think of your soul as constantly sending messages to your mind about your spiritual reality and the power of your true being. Yet, these messages are often lost beneath the avalanche of thoughts about the material aspect of life, which has created a busy and superficial mind, frenetically racing through the day, believing that working hard to get through the "to do" list will bring happiness and success.

Unity and conscious contact means that, as you become whole, your inside and outside selves become one and the same because your soul is now the overwhelming presence in your life. At first, conscious contact usually happens only during your specific time of meditation, for example in the morning and evening—this is where the lower self makes conscious contact with the higher self. As you continue your practice, you will develop a stronger relationship between these two aspects of the self. As this happens, the presence of the higher self is naturally maintained as you arise from meditation and continue your day. One of the wisdoms in meditating twice a day, once in the morning and once in the evening, is that you are creating powerful cognitive links in the neural networks of your brain and body. Reinforcing these links in your brain twice a day significantly increases your success rate in achieving your goals and manifesting the life upon which you are focusing. Just imagine if you wanted to learn a new language and you studied once a week—progress would be slow. However, if you immersed yourself in the culture of the language, your progress would grow exponentially. This is what you are doing by meditating twice a day and then extending the meditation into your day—you are immersing yourself in a new cultural reality, a culture that you are creating.

The brain's quality of neuroplasticity is its beautiful capacity to literally change its form and structure to accommodate new patterns of activity. From your very first meditation, your brain will respond with its flexible dynamic, taking you closer to where you orient your attention. Even if there is some neural rigidity to overcome from years of being in a cognitive rut, when you regularly meditate, morning and evening, the new patterns of meditative activity become more powerful than the old ways of thinking, feeling, believing, and acting. Truly, not only can you change your mind; you can also transform your life with consistent and soulful meditation.

Being conscious of and living from your soul is a process, which at a certain point in life becomes a constant and sacred way of being in the world. This way of being is categorically distinct from making conscious contact only during meditation or other temporary experiences. It is a continual state of awareness and of being in touch with your soul. Rather than only meditating as a separate part of your life, your life becomes a meditation, an experience often called mindfulness.

Moving from the stage of making conscious contact during meditation to the stage of living meditation is like being totally revivified, awakened from a deep sleep, or reborn. Your life is recreated and you become aware of an indissoluble bond with the source of all things that brought you forth from the realm of the unmanifest into this life of the manifest. Rather than "thinking" as you used to about any given subject or question, your thinking becomes spiritualized, arising from your soul, manifested in your mind, and then expressed through your behavior and energies. This is the state where, in addition to your individual meditations, life itself is meditation. It is where, in addition to your private prayers, life itself is a prayer, where you no longer simply "do beautiful acts," but your life itself is beauty, diffusing the sweet-scented fragrance of love and light at all times and under all conditions.

In this state, you see people as souls, spiritual beings with a covering we call the body and personality. When you interact with another soul, you are aware that you are both part of a great web of life, interconnected and whole. You embody and manifest human virtues in balanced measure for any situation that might arise and in any capacity you might serve, whether in your job, as a parent, a child, a friend, or as a member of your particular family, neighborhood, or the global community.

Experiencing Meditation

Can you imagine wanting to be an Olympic swimmer, but limiting your training program to merely reading books and articles about swimming and never once getting into the pool? The key to learning anything and mastering it is experience—if you want to learn to swim, you have to get wet! If you want to master your life, you have to submerge yourself in the limitless ocean of your soul. Until you experience it, it is impossible to appreciate the powerful influence that the soul or higher self can exercise in your life. To get a better sense of certain aspects of your attention and consciousness and how they shape your life, let's look at a few typical experiences.

Universal Experiences

In my research, all participants have had similar experiences where their attention, seemingly of its own volition, connects to a greater consciousness which some describe as a collective or universal consciousness, or spiritual reality. Consider this common experience of attention. Have you ever read a paragraph, perhaps even a page or two of a book, and then realized that although your eyes were moving across the page, your mind was elsewhere? Perhaps when you attempt to reread the same section, you have the same experience of your attention being on something else, or being somewhere else. When you shake yourself out of that state and again focus your attention to try and read the pages of the book, you likely don't remember where your attention was or what you were thinking about. When this happens, it is as though your mind secretly drifts away from your conscious awareness—a kind of mental vacation from the rest of the world, a special state of consciousness that is quiet, still, at peace, and in its natural state—a type of meditative state. In such moments, your body is still, at peace, relaxed, almost nonexistent. Like your mind, your body is also in a special state of consciousness, a unique kind of awareness—at one with the universe. Your mind and body are not only in unity with each other at such times, they are in a state of communication with your soul, the vital force that animates them. I call this special state of being your sacred consciousness, sacred awareness, or sacred thought.

Another common experience during spiritual thought is expressed as gazing off into the distance. When this happens, you are looking at nothing in particular, though your eyes are often fixed, focused, and taking in everything in your field of vision. This is a kind of open-eyed meditation, where you are gazing into the distance but not intending to look at any one thing to examine its qualities, its color, shape, or size. Your mind is absorbed in another subject, which is usually beyond words. You have likely experienced this when, for instance, a friend who was just talking to you sees that you have drifted off to another place and says to you, "Hello! Are you listening? What were you thinking about?" and you cannot express it in words. This is perfectly natural, since the spiritual state of mind you were just inhabiting was transcendent to language. It was a private conversation between you and your soul self that was conducted in silence, without the often cumbersome tool of language.

Perhaps a more powerful experience to which all people can relate is that of the dream state. Like the examples above, a dream state is a specialized state of consciousness. In a dream, we can experience anything we desire or need. In dreams we can fly, create, experience rebirth or death, be rich or poor, relive the past, or see into the future. We can also experience a profound level of oneness with other people and all of nature that seems impossible during our waking life.

It is telling and paradoxical that making conscious contact with and experiencing the power of the soul often happens in the dream state, while one is asleep. Sleep often removes the barrier of the physical self and quiets the chatter of the lower self. For most people, the lower self is far too present in their minds, and its constant attention to the world and the daily concerns of life brings nothing but stress, sadness, or false sense of joy and fulfillment. In sleep, the lower self is often quieted—it is as though when the physical self sleeps, so does the lower self, and the spiritual self wakes up. The soul never sleeps or goes away, it is always present; a lower state of consciousness just covers it up.

It might seem counterintuitive to think that something like the soul, which is eternal and incredibly powerful, can be covered up by silly, fleeting, or lower-level thoughts. But consider how a single cloud or thin eyelid can block out the powerful light of the sun; or how a tiny speck of dust can severely reduce the function of your eyes. When you fall asleep, it is like the dust is removed from the eyes, or the cloud moves away from the sun, and the powerful presence of the higher self simply emerges into the forefront of conscious awareness and finally has the opportunity to be fully active.

To use a musical metaphor, it is as though your soul is a beautiful, powerful, and inspiring song that is always playing; yet the noise of the lower self is so loud that you can't hear your soul's song. However, once the noise of the lower self is turned off, the soul music rings out and carries you to the height of spiritual ecstasy. Although sleep can often turn off the noise of the lower self, what happens when you wake up and the noise of the lower self returns? Here is where music and meditation can help. Through your meditation practice, you will be able to silence the noise of the lower self during wakefulness. Music and meditation provide ways to experience and become more familiar with your soul self without falling asleep. By keeping both the physical and spiritual aspects of your being awake, and by increasing the conscious presence of your soul during wakefulness, a process of transformation begins that is nothing short of miraculous. Just as you have likely had certain beautiful and miraculous dreams, waking life will become imbued with the same power of your soul, creating the life that can be limited only by your imagination.

Spiritual Cognition and Imagination

Here we begin to enter the spiritual cognitive dimension of transformation. Imagination is one aspect of creating what you want, first by imagining it in your mind, and then by experiencing it as real and true in your meditation. Often, imagination is not a problem for people. Rather, the next critical steps of fully believing in your meditation, seeing it as real, and then living as though it already exists are what must be done. In dreams, this process is collapsed into simultaneity, where an imagination is instantaneously experienced as real.

In dreams, the borders between the self and everything else in the physical world are fuzzy, blurred, or at times simply not there, so there is an instantaneous dynamic between having a desire and manifesting it. This experience of having a desire and manifesting it immediately, without any time lag, is called a quantum event. A quantum event occurs in a pure and natural state of consciousness, when the mind is totally peaceful and in a state of oneness. This state of oneness is a level within your consciousness and can be accessed and developed through music and meditation. In this specialized state of being, you are able to manifest everything your heart desires. Moreover, this state is a window into your soul, your noble higher self, the self that is more powerful than the universe, the self that is beyond physical illness, the self that is always happy, radiant, joyful, laughing, flying high, alive, energetic, and eternal.

Your soul, your true self, is beyond description through language since, by definition, it is beyond the attributes of the physical universe. Nevertheless, the universe provides many profound and beautiful metaphors and examples for understanding the qualities of the soul. These help us gain insight into our true nature and unlimited potential. There is an ancient Chinese saying that always reminds me of one of the qualities of the soul: Be still as a mountain, move like a great river. When you are still, things flow, answers come from your soul to your mind, the path clears and a way is found. During a dream, the body is still, asleep, yet the invisible and eternal part of yourself can walk on water, fly above the treetops, talk to another soul that has passed away, or visit with friends in New York, Delhi, Beijing, and Barcelona all in the span of a few seconds!

Go for a Visit

Consciously getting in contact with your soul is like visiting a wise and loving friend whose door is always open and who always has the perfect answer to any question. It is as though your wise soul self lives in a tree house where the breeze blows gently and the buds blossom with beautiful, fragrant flowers and bear luscious fruits. Your daily self lives in a house on the ground and can't reach life in the tree house— you need a ladder to ascend upward. Music and meditation are your ladders. You use them to climb up to make contact with your own soul. Once you have an experience with your soul, that place of quantum events, total health, peace, certitude, joy, and power, you are changed forever—you are refreshed, renewed, and recreated. As you visit with your soul every morning and evening inside meditation, you begin to take on the qualities of your soul more and more outside of meditation and your life inside and outside of meditation become one.

For example, if your lower self has doubt, when you visit your soul self in meditation in the morning, the doubt dissolves in the presence of the beauty, strength, and certitude of your soul. After your morning meditation, the doubt might return, but not to worry—this is very normal and you will learn in the next chapter how to turn that doubt into certitude outside of meditation. As you continue your meditation practice morning and evening, you become more and more like your soul until it is fully present in your heart and mind that the doubt will not return ever again. You will know that you are eternal and can manifest all the virtues and realities that you can imagine.

Music and Meditation

Music and meditation have been used as ladders to communicate with the soul throughout the ages and across all cultures of the world. They are expressed with infinite diversity and form a universal phenomenon in the human experience. A music student once asked me how it is that sometimes, when she is totally in the music, she will play things on her instrument that she could never conceive of before, something totally fresh and new, never before possible to her.

This experience never comes for her at the beginning of a musical event or practice. It always takes some time to get into the music, to climb the ladder, to immerse herself in a specialized soundscape and an altered or extraordinary state of consciousness. This altered mental state is akin to the dream state, a place ripe with potential for quantum events. In this state of consciousness, the daily self that seems to be separate from the rest of the world becomes the higher self, which is in full unity with the universe and can therefore manifest anything it desires that is part of the universe.

This student, at the subtlest level of her consciousness, desires to manifest music that she has never known or experienced before. Then, without any delay, the music is instantaneously manifested; without thinking about what to play, the music flows from the universe through her and her instrument, vibrating the airwaves in the room she is in. The airwaves then vibrate against her tympanic membrane, which vibrates the bones of the inner ear, and are carried by the eighth cranial nerve directly into the brain, which brings a momentary experience of bliss. This moment of bliss, which is a combination of unlimited and intoxicating levels of love, joy, transcendence, oneness, power, and radiance, is a tangible experience of her soul self.

Using music for meditation is like being a wakeful dreamer. Music helps you to enter a kind of daydreaming state wherein you can plant the seed of your most desired life. You can imagine total health, prosperity, joy, and beauty in all aspects of life and experience it within your musical world, knowing it to be true and real. Then, after your musical meditation, you continue in that state of knowing to further experience the inside state of meditation in the outside world of daily activity. Morning to evening and evening to morning, little by little and day by day, your life becomes the reality that you imagine and experience in your meditative mind.

What is the greatest desire deep in your heart and at the forefront of your mind? How can you live in the state of higher consciousness? How can you facilitate quantum events of manifesting your deepest desires, creating happiness, health, and wealth in your life? How, then, can you let that joyful, healing energy flow out to everyone whom you contact daily, eventually letting your unending soul energy of joy, radiance, power, and healing flow to all humanity?

If you climb the ladder of music and meditation daily, if you experience the soul energy of your sacred thought when you get to the top of the ladder, you will be well on your way to a new life of happiness, health, wealth, fulfillment, peace, power, and energy. The only thing left to do will be to carry the essence of the experience you have at the top of the ladder into your daily actions. Before you know it, not only will your daily life begin to change, naturally reflecting your higher self in all you do, but you will become lighter, more carefree and clear-minded, stronger, gentler, wiser, more prosperous, and happier. You will develop an openness and acceptance of others, a sincere and profound love of life and all people, a compassion and empathy for people at all stages of life, a respect and reverence for yourself and the soul of each person. Day by day, you will become more thankful for everything great and small that is in your life, and you will long to manifest love at every moment. With every breath, you will seek to encourage yourself and others. You will bring clarity, love, and light to each and every occasion.

Thoughts to Remember from This Chapter

I am a spiritual being; my soul is my true and eternal self—
I Am Soul.

My soul is only positive, therefore any negative qualities I
have are not essentially my self, but rather my lower self;
they are temporary, and naturally fade away as I meditate
and extend the focus of my meditation into my day.

Through music and meditation, my higher self becomes more
and more present as the real and only me. As this happens,
the lower self gently fades away.

My thoughts and actions create my reality.

Music and meditation are ladders that enable me to go
beyond any limitation, immerse myself in the purifying
energy of my soul, and create the life that I desire.

As this happens, I begin to automatically view all life
experiences

in a new and positive light.

My thoughts, decisions, and actions progressively create more
happiness, health, and wealth in my life.

CHAPTER 6

The Power of Music, Sound, and Meditation

Music carries the soul's inspiration into manifestation.

~

Five Factors: Physical, Psychological, Social, Emotional, Spiritual

What is it about music, specialized sound, and meditation that is especially effective in facilitating higher consciousness, happiness, health, and wealth? The answer to this question lies in what I call the Five Factors: the Physical, Psychological, Social, Emotional, and Spiritual aspects of music and meditation. Importantly, these are the same Five Factors that constitute health and healing and which comprise a human being. That is to say, since music and meditation, health and healing, happiness and wealth, and a human being all have these Five Factors in common, the more you understand and experience how music and meditation engage these factors, the more you can facilitate a holistic transformation across these five domains of life.

A key concept here is that the Physical, Psychological, Social, Emotional, and Spiritual are more than just aspects, domains, or dimensions of life; they are factors, or active components, that must be engaged and factored into life to create transformation. Figure 3 models the Five Factors in the following areas: A Human Being; Music and Meditation; Health and Healing; and Happiness and Wealth. This is a holistic model that highlights the interconnectedness and dynamic influence of its components.

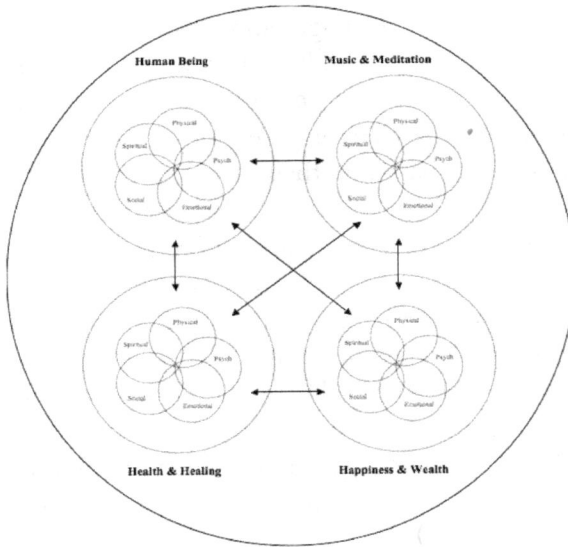

Figure 3: Interrelationships of the Five Factors

Figure 3 shows that a Human Being, Music & Meditation, Health & Healing, and Happiness & Wealth all share the exact same factors. To understand the multiple relationships among these factors, we can imagine four identical spheres that overlay each other. They are transparent and have the Five Factors—physical, psychological, social, emotional, and spiritual, written on their surface.

The words float across the surface and through the bodies of the spheres in a free-flowing manner, never being fixed in one place. The most important aspect of this holistic model is that each factor can transform into other factors.

So, imagine that that you are holding these four spheres in your hands and that they overlay each other in such a way that they form one sphere with four translucent layers; yet, because they are identical, the four seeming layers strangely form one whole. Each of the spheres has a distinct individual motion, spinning, swirling, and rotating on its own, yet a complementary relationship can be seen among them as they also form a coherent whole. Variable speeds and directions can be seen in the movement of the spheres, and the dynamism of the interaction among and within the spheres shows the complex nature of their functions.

Now, imagine that when an effectual relationship is created among factors, for instance if the emotional factor of a particular piece of music effects a change in the psychological factor of your being, which has an impact on the physical factor of health, which then influences your relationships, a link or thread is illumined in the model where this occurs. Subsequently, according to the strength of that association and the action of the spheres' rotation and dynamism, the illumined link or thread is spun throughout all regions of the model, interweaving itself with all the factors of music and meditation, your being, health and healing, and your happiness and wealth. Keep in mind that, although the initial link was made between specific factors, the model allows for the factors to transform into other factors to show their holistic nature. So, as the physical effect in the health and healing sphere rotates, the physical factor slowly transforms into one or more of the other factors, each with the potential to create new efficacious links, which effects further transformations in the whole.

The central point to convey here is that, by engaging any one of the factors, you have the potential to effect a transformation in any of the other factors present in any area of life, and, most importantly, in life as a whole. Figure 4 shows the intimately and inextricably interwoven nature of the relationships between the factors of music and meditation with the other areas of life. While the image implies direct links across all dimensions, it is important to note that they function through a non-linear, quantum dynamic, which I explain further below.

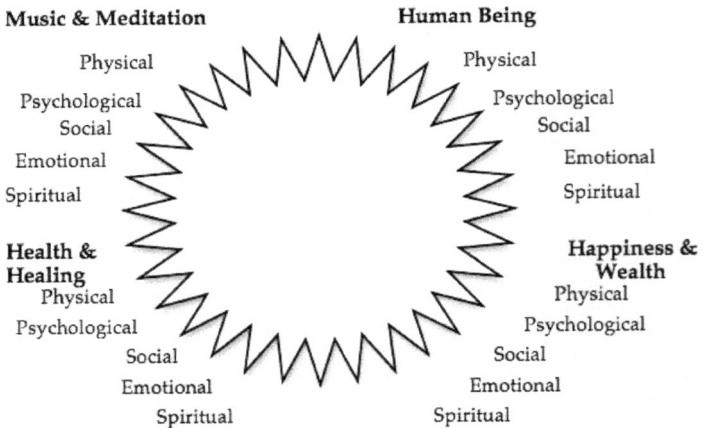

Music & Meditation   **Human Being**
Physical   Physical
Psychological   Psychological
Social   Social
Emotional   Emotional
Spiritual   Spiritual

Health &   **Happiness &**
Healing   **Wealth**
Physical   Physical
Psychological   Psychological
Social   Social
Emotional   Emotional
Spiritual   Spiritual

Figure 4: Interconnectedness

Figure 4 highlights the interconnectedness of the Five Factors of music and meditation with the factors of a human being, happiness and prosperity, and health and healing. Following the pattern already illustrated here, there are implied connections between all the factors whereby a change in one can effect a transformation in the whole. It is important to note that the Five Factors represent aspects of one unified whole, not five separate unrelated domains. They are facets that provide insight into the rich and beautiful expression of a balanced and whole life.

It is no coincidence that these dimensions not only relate to sound, music, and meditation, but are also fully interwoven with our consciousness, happiness, health, and prosperity. Through your individual practice of meditation, you will develop the capacity to make any experience a ladder to a higher reality, where every moment, whether in meditation, conversation, play, prayer, cooking, working, or anything else, becomes a means of moving into a higher spiritual consciousness. When you are steadfast in this new state of being, you become like a magnet, attracting exactly what you need into your life at any given moment.

In my own experience, the passionate will to put into action the principles and practices in this book have transformed my life in countless ways. Even writing this book has been a personally rewarding and healing experience, bringing me in closer contact with my soul. For example, when I awoke at three o'clock this morning, inspired to continue writing this book, my soul spoke to me this essence of what it means to transform through meditation. It said:

All you have to do is think of me—
your soul, the light of unity within your heart.
I am with you and in you always, at all times and
under all conditions.
Whatever you need, I can provide.
All you have to do is turn your thoughts to me,
and let your consciousness flow through
all aspects of your being.
I am ever whispering in your heart and mind,
that your true reality is eternal, spiritual,

that you are soul, pure, love, peace, strength,
health, joy, wealth, and beauty. We are one.

Experiencing the Power of Meditation

When you meditate, you become aware of the source of your being, which is the source of all of creation—a source that is all-loving and powerful, ever-present and ready to respond to an open and creative heart. This source is like a limitless river that flows into any vessel that is open. In that rarefied atmosphere of spiritual consciousness, your true nature illuminates all aspects of your being and all things become possible. In meditation, you realize that you are an eternal spiritual being with the ability to create the life you can imagine and, in the silent beauty of your meditative mind, you are in perfect health, full of joy, strength, certitude, wealth, and peace.

You might be wondering, "If, outside of meditation, I am sick, angry, sad, depressed, stressed, or in need of money, what real good can meditation bring to me to actually change my situation?" To fully appreciate the power of the experience of meditation, we must first consider the role that experience plays in our lives.

First, consider that every experience in your life has brought you to the place you are now, even to this very moment of reading the words on the pages of this book. Then, consider how certain experiences that you have had in the past have profoundly influenced your life or changed it totally. Even one experience, one moment, or one decision can shape all subsequent experiences in life. Finally, consider how the repetition of a particular experience (or practice) can do the same—entirely transform your life. When we repeat certain actions, we literally create and recreate ourselves in every aspect. In a very real way, we become what we focus our attention on.

In a benchmark work in cognitive science that views meditation as an essential aspect of scientific inquiry and experience as a key to enact (create) the world one desires, Francisco Varela and his colleagues drew upon a classic study by Held and Hein:

"These researchers raised kittens in the dark and exposed them to light only under controlled conditions. A first group of animals was allowed to move around normally, but each of them was harnessed to a simple carriage and basket that contained a number of the second group of kittens. The two groups therefore shared the same visual experience, but the second group was entirely passive. When the animals were released after a few weeks of this treatment, the first group of kittens behaved normally, but those who had been carried around behaved as if they were blind: they bumped into

objects and fell over edges."

What their study shows is that the physical sense of vision is not dependent on the eyes alone, but on the experience of interacting with the world. Without experience, the kittens would have remained blind.

Using this as a model, consider the faculty of inner vision that one cultivates in meditation. If you have never interacted with that inner landscape of the meditative mind and connection to your soul, then you could remain blind and, like the kittens, bump into things, stumble, and fall. But for you it would not be bumping into objects or falling over things, but stumbling or falling over the psychological and emotional tests of life. Most important is that this study also shows that, through a new experience, blindness can change into sight! All you need to do is cultivate your experience in the inner landscape of your meditative mind. If you are experiencing illness, stress, anger, or sadness outside of meditation, you are like the kittens that were raised in the dark. But, by visiting your soul self through your meditative mind and having an experience there, that place of inner vision and light, your outside experience (like the blind kittens) begins to transform. You become like the kittens, once they were free to interact with their environment. You become the master of your life.

Transforming the Meditative Mind into Matter

One of the great scientists of the last century was Max Planck, a Nobel laureate in physics, who, along with

Einstein, Neils Bohr, Werner Heisenberg, and other physicists of the time, pioneered early developments in quantum physics, which views the particles of an atom not as solid matter but as fluctuations of waves of energy that are potentially manifest as material substance. Planck, in expressing the profound nature of the elusive and invisible link between the unmanifest and manifest, made this remarkable statement in a 1944 lecture in Florence, Italy:

"As a man who has devoted his whole life to the most clear-headed science, to the study of matter, I can tell you as the result of my research about atoms, this much—there is no matter as such. All matter originates and exists only by virtue of a force, which brings the particles of an atom to vibration and holds this most minute solar system of the atom together. We must assume behind this force the existence of a conscious and intelligent mind. This mind is the matrix of all matter."

At the heart of this statement is a premise from quantum mechanics that led Plank and others, in their clear-headed and scientific attempts to pierce the mysteries of matter, to conclude that there is something else that cannot be described by the terms thing, matter, or physical, but which is, by definition, metaphysical. Drawing from this statement, if M=mind/matrix of all matter, F=force, p=particles, A=atom, and m=matter, then we can represent the process as shown in Figure 5.

$$(p)\,A$$

$$M \mid F \rightleftharpoons m$$

Figure 5: Mind to Matter

Further, if we view the same process with different terms, we can discern aspects of the model to highlight the role of an individual's thought or cognition in a personal process of transformation and creating a new reality. Hence, M (mind/ matrix of all matter) can also be viewed as the universal mind, the unified field, the collective unconscious; and F (force) is a person's thought. Additionally, M can refer to higher consciousness and F to present or lower consciousness, between which there is a two-way connection. This connection forms a bridge or ladder whereby energy can be transferred between the two. This ladder that connects the lower consciousness with the higher consciousness can help us to understand the nature of the mystical mechanics whereby generative and transforming energy can flow between the metaphysical realm that is the matrix of all matter and the personal mind, from which projections of energy waves that we call thoughts play a central role in creating particles of happiness, health, and wealth. Figure 6 shows this process as a transformation from the lower self or Lower Consciousness to the higher self or Higher Consciousness.

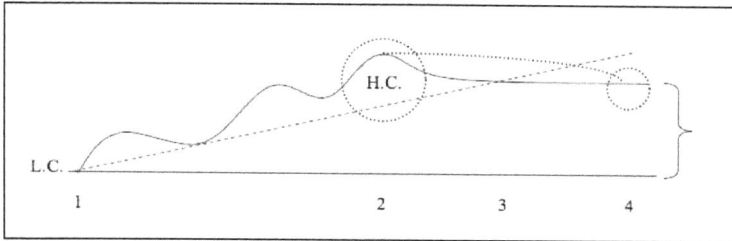

Figure 6: Transformation of Consciousness

In Figure 6, the numbers 1, 2, 3, and 4 indicate points in time. Number 1 marks the beginning your meditative practice; number 2 indicates the highest point of meditation where you have the real experience of that which is the focus of your attention; and number 3 signals the end of the meditation session. Number 4 is a special moment during your daily activities where you recall the high point of meditation to literally bring the power of that experience to the present moment and imbue whatever you are doing in he here and now with the qualities and realities of your meditation.

L.C. stands for Lower Consciousness and H.C. for Higher Consciousness. In addition to showing the movement from the lower to higher consciousness, the figure also represents the transformation in one or more of the Five Factors—the body, mind, emotions, social dynamics, and spiritual capacities.

The dashed line that extends from the lower left corner of the graphic to the upper right represents any practice (for example, music, meditation, breathing, prayer, dance, movement) that forms a ladder or channel between the L.C. and H.C. The solid wavy line represents one example of the attention of a practitioner, showing a general pattern that often occurs; that is, in the beginning there is often a fluctuation in the mind's attention when moving toward the Higher Consciousness—it can go up and down a bit as it moves forward. This is normal and decreases as you practice. The more you meditate and practice the steps outlined in the coming chapters, the more your meditation will build momentum and move more steadily upward.

The dotted circle around the H.C. indicates the empowered experience that occurs at the height of the meditative practice. Most important in the graphic is the section of the solid wavy line after the meditation has ended, from point 3 to point 4. Notice that the line, which represents consciousness, gently descends and levels out after the highpoint of the meditation has been experienced. From point 3 to point 4, consciousness is maintained at a level that is less than the apex of the experience shown at point 2, but much higher than that of the L.C., at point 1. The bracket on the right illustrates the degree of transformation that has occurred. This can also be seen as a change in the quality of awareness that has moved from a lower stage to a higher one through the dynamics and capacities of cognitive flexibility, neuroplasticity, entrainment, embeingment, and the experience of certainty described by the HCP, the Human Certainty Principle.

The goal of the meditation is to extend the spirit or essence of the experience of the H.C. past point 3, imbuing all of life with that energy, including your next session of meditation (see Figure 7). The second, smaller circle that appears at point 4 is a reflection of the larger circle around the H.C. and shows that when you turn your attention to your true self that you have come to know during the experience of the high point of meditation, you can be your true self throughout your daily experience. The dotted arced line between the two circles represents a cognitive link or personal reminder between the experience of the H.C. and your daily experience—it is a reminder about your true soul self. This link or reminder often takes the form of you directly recalling the focus of your meditation.

For example, if you focused on "strength and courage" in your meditation, these words and the feelings of strength and courage that you experienced during your meditation can be a cognitive link, a reminder of your true experience of total strength and courage during the high point of your meditation. Throughout your day, after your morning meditation, whenever you need the experience of strength and courage, you can, in the moment, close your eyes for a few seconds while taking a deep breath, giving it your full attention, and recall or say, "Strength, courage," silently or aloud, and you will immediately revisit your high point of meditation and re-experience a degree of your power from meditation.

The following chapters explain this technique in more detail. What is important here is for you to know that you have the power to create exactly what you need throughout the day and that your meditation is your storehouse of power and energy for any situation. In addition, the sense and reality of "strength and courage" or "health" or anything that you focus on in your meditation can emerge indirectly, through no direct attempt on your part to recall it. This is yet another aspect of the impact of meditation on your life. Whatever is the focus of your meditation will, day by day, become more the focus of your daily life in subtle and pronounced ways, which you will experience in all Five Factors of your being.

Look again at points 3 and 4 in the figure above. This shows your state of being after meditation and throughout your day, which is higher than when you began your meditation but not quite as high as the total experience of your higher self at point 2 in the figure. Nevertheless, the next time you meditate, your starting point for climbing the ladder of meditation will be higher than the starting point of your previous meditation. So, you can see that there is a cyclic progression of ascending the ladder of meditation, which builds from session to session and from day to day. Figure 7 shows this cycle with two meditation sessions, one in the morning and one in the evening.

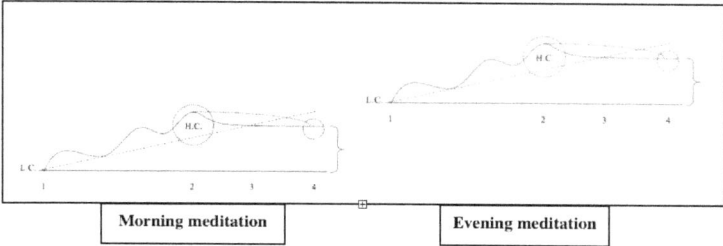

Figure 7: Morning and Evening
Cycles of Meditation

In the above figure, you can see that the evening meditation starts where the morning meditation ended. This general principle is then extended from session to session, day to day, week to week, month to month, and year to year. It is just like the principle of practicing any skill: with each practice session, one improves and grows in capacity. In meditation, you will also grow and develop, increase your capacity, and create new and wonderful realities in your life.

CHAPTER 7

Good Vibrations

*All matter originates and exists only by virtue of a force,
which brings the particles of an atom to vibration
and holds this most minute solar system of the atom together.
We must assume behind this force
the existence of a conscious and intelligent mind.
This mind is the matrix of all matter.*
–Max Planck

All Things Are in Vibration

Have you ever felt in tune with yourself and others, in your body and thoughts, your emotional heart, and even your soul? Have you ever felt out of tune or out of sync with yourself or others? These experiences can be understood by the principles of vibration we will discuss here. As we learn a bit more about their nature and potential influence, you will grow in your understanding and appreciation of the power of music, your mind, and meditation to tune your being and create the desired state.

There is a law and principle of nature that underlies the power that exists among the Five Factors of music and the Five Factors of your being. Understanding this natural principle and law will help you to engage your meditation practice to create health and healing, happiness, higher consciousness, wealth, and prosperity. The law is that all things are in vibration, and the principle is that balance equals health, happiness, progress, and wealth; and imbalance equals illness, loss, and degeneration. Moreover, creating a balanced state of vibration also relates to manifesting the desires of your heart in any aspect of life. So, when one's vibratory state is balanced in all the Five Factors, the result is happiness, health, and wealth.

Each and every thing or entity has a healthy or balanced state of vibration. So, if imbalance occurs in one's being, this can also be understood as an imbalance in the one's vibratory state or resonance. You can think of your vibratory state as being like an instrument that is either in tune or out of tune. The process of tuning your being can be seen to cross all factors on a nonlinear continuum of energy. Here, vibration is not just the physical energy that can be measured, but higher spiritual frequencies that are beyond the capacity of physical measurement. Musicians and healers steeped in ancient wisdom have long known this truth, which is an accepted precept in quantum physics: that from the invisible world of dancing subatomic waves and particles to the infinite expanses of space, all things are in vibration. Moreover, we are part of that field of vibration and can effect change therein. Following this thought, we can say that the vibration of health will be different than that of illness.

Going one step further, we can say that health, happiness, and higher consciousness can be seen as balanced vibration, and illness, disease, and lower consciousness as imbalanced vibration, or vibration moving away from its balanced state.

In other words, every physical thing has a particular vibratory state or spectrum of vibrations that defines its optimal or healthy state, which we can say is balanced or in tune. When the vibrations of that healthy state change enough, the healthy state also changes to one of dis-ease, imbalance, or being out of tune. Building from the natural law of entrainment, it follows that there is a potential to steer an imbalanced or out-of-tune vibratory state back to balance either by directly introducing that object's natural or healthy state of vibration or by gradually moving toward the healthy vibratory state. Most important is that the process of tuning or balancing yourself is not just a physical process; it is one that relates to all Five Factors—your body, mind, spirit, emotions, and relationships.

Sound, Music, and Vibration

Vibrations are ever-present in our environment. Some vibrations or frequencies are beyond our spectrum of hearing, either too high or too low, but they can still have an effect on our beings. The vibrations that we can hear we simply call sound. However, sound is anything but simple when we consider the power and meaning that it can carry. Although sound and music are vibrations of energy carried through the air, when they are in sync with your optimal and natural vibratory state, they have the power to change imbalance to balance, to effect healing transformations in your being, to move your heart and soul, and to create a clear and wonderful mind. Just think of how you respond to the sound of the voice of someone you love, the calming effect it can have or the joy it can engender. Or think of a song that immediately brings memories and emotions from the distant past flashing to the forefront of your heart and mind, perhaps bringing forth tears, laughter, compassion, or a deep sense of thankfulness. When the vibrations of a sound, voice, song, or music are in sync with your personal vibratory state, or when they engender a level of vibration that you need to balance or tune your being, the results can range from the slight benefit of an emotional boost to a seemingly miraculous transformation or manifestation.

Conversely, when vibrations are out of sync with an object's natural state, they can bring about illness and destruction. Consider the classic example of the physical power of sound shattering a glass. Even an unamplified singer's voice can create enough vibrating sound energy to negatively affect the resonance frequencies of the glass until it breaks down. This is a profound example of how vibration in sound and music can create a serious imbalance in the physical makeup of the glass. The power of the singer's voice is too much for the glass to withstand and the vibration of the voice overwhelms, transforms, and destroys the glass.

What then are the balancing effects of vibrations on your body and in the rest of your being, including your thoughts, emotions, spirit, and personal relationships? Answers to these questions can be very personal, and reflecting on them can enable you to harness the power of sound and music for meditation and your life.

Vibration and Meaning

Aspects of Vibration

Typically, scientists consider only five of the six aspects of vibration or sound: duration, direction, amplitude, waveform, and frequency. The sixth however, is the most important for higher consciousness, happiness, health, and wealth. This sixth aspect is meaning. Moreover, conventional scientific perspectives do not explore these aspects in relation to happiness, health, and wealth. So, a brief description follows here that will further expand your understanding of the potential transformative powers of sound and music.

Duration is the time measurement of a sound from beginning to end. It is powerful in transforming the mind, generating happiness, and promoting healing when it is expressed as a long extended tone or drone, as is found in many types of healing music. In my sound/music healing practice, I employ and teach many approaches that include long extended tones that create a generative and transformative space. In this special sound space, profound experiences of transformation and healing can occur. The practices I employ include long tone vocalization, chanting, didgeridoo resonance healing, specialized drumming, and other sounds and music created and performed specifically for individuals according to their particular needs.

Direction refers to the place of the sound source—a voice, an instrument, nature, and speakers or headphones for recorded music. However, there is also a metaphysical meaning when viewed from the perspective that the spiritual dimension is often the source of healing sounds. For example, in traditional Lakota culture, dreams are often a direct expression of the spiritual realm from which songs and music emerge and are given to the dreamer as a sacred trust. In traditional Pamiri culture in the mountains known as the roof of the world, the rubab (long-necked lute) is viewed as a spiritual instrument that is especially used for devotional music and healing. There are also specialized instruments across world cultures that are given spiritual meaning and are seen to connect one with the Source of creation.

Amplitude is the scientific term for the degree of energy in a sound, which we perceive as volume and which we experience as the degree of loudness of a sound. It also indicates the degree of pressure created by a vibration or oscillator. Amplitude is a category to measure the physical power of sound and music. Consider the effect that loud music has on you. Sometimes it can be extremely irritating, but sometimes it can increase your strength and energy to an incredible degree and help you to accomplish feats you might not otherwise be able to do. It is precisely for this reason that certain loud music, which carries the intended meaning, is performed at sporting events: to increase adrenaline and literally get people pumped up into a heightened state of physical power. In many cultures, volume is an important component of music to achieve specific outcomes, including transformation and healing.

Waveform refers to the shape of a sound wave and the tonal qualities it expresses. We experience this as timbre or tone color. This means that we can hear distinctive qualities within sound. A sound can be dark, bright, edgy, airy, smooth, rough, soft, hard, round, full, hollow, nasal, deep, and so forth. The specific quality of a sound is key to creating emotional responses in your heart that are then carried throughout your body and being.

Frequency refers to the number of repetitions of a waveform per unit of time. In other words, frequency measures how frequently a waveform repeats itself in a certain time period. Frequency is expressed in terms of Hz (hertz). Hertz is a measurement of the number of cycles per second of a waveform. We experience frequency as the highness or lowness of a sound, which we call pitch perception. In a similar way, this plays into our emotional experience of what we hear. Pitch also relates to your chakra energy centers, and your awareness of this can help you to sense the relationships between different pitches and specific chakras.

Finally, and most importantly, meaning refers to what a sound or music carries into your being (your heart, mind, body, and spirit), including all of the associations that are inherent or given to all levels of vibration, sound, and music. The reason that meaning is so important for the 5 Steps is that you will have the opportunity to create the exact meaning that you choose to incorporate into your being and your life through your meditation practice.

Aspects of Meaning

There are two kinds of meaning that we will discuss here: inherent meaning and given meaning. Inherent meaning is the meaning that already exists in a sound or music and which is culture-transcendent or universal. Given meaning is meaning that you assign to a particular sound or music. These are not necessarily mutually exclusive, but just a way to explore sound and meaning and prepare you for the exercises that you will begin in chapter 9.

Some examples will be helpful here. In the ancient Indian concept of the anahata nada or "unstruck" sound, there is an inherent meaning of an ever-present sound, without beginning or end. This meaning is also adopted and given by individuals in their experience and practice of spiritual sounds, music, and in meditation, since one's experience is often that of timelessness, placelessness, and transcendence.

A beautiful example of an inherent-given meaning of sound, which is also associated with ancient India, is the empowering and creative sound of AUM (or OM). This sound is a vital force expressive of a spiritual reality, of oneness, wholeness, and wellness. It is from this spiritual reality that the physical world and all of creation was manifested. When you make such a sound with your voice, you immediately become more relaxed, less stressed, happier, stronger, and more oriented toward health.

In a categorically different example, have you ever experienced a door slamming shut with a loud bang? This sound also has an inherent quality to it. Consider, even if you are aware that a loud bang is about to happen when the door slams, and even if you are looking at the door, you will still respond immediately when it happens. Typical experiences include galvanic skin response, commonly called goose bumps, a tightening of blood vessels (vasoconstriction), increased blood pressure, and an orienting response in the brain.

There are many examples of how sound and music can effect change, both positively and negatively. Here, we are focusing on the positive and creative aspects of sound and music that you can learn and practice to create the life you desire. Nevertheless, it is critically important for you to also be aware of the negative effects of sound and music that are carried both by vibrations and meaning. This is true for people of all ages and cultures. The impact of music is immediately felt in your being—in your body, gut, heart, mind, and how you relate to other people. For example, if the frequency (pitch) and waveforms (tone color/timbre) of a person's voice seem to just rub you the wrong way and is not related to the content of what they say, then there is either a meaning in the sound itself or a clashing of the voice with your inner ear's hearing mechanism, although the latter is extremely rare.

A more common example builds from the metaphor of being a music consumer and the notion of you are what you eat. That is, listening to music is similar to eating or consuming food. The difference is that, with music, you take in or consume it with your ears, mind, heart, body, and soul, rather than just your mouth. If, for example, a child listens to or consumes negative, violent, or degrading messages in music, this meaning will slowly become part of that child's mindset, worldview, beliefs, and identity. Behaviors then follow what is in the child's mind. This is the central problem with much of today's popular music. For instance, the meaning carried in much of today's popular music and videos is an expression of the lower self and ego consciousness that conveys inequality and injustice between women and men, exalts and even idolizes the material, physical, and sexual aspects of life, and is largely devoid of references to our inherent spiritual reality. Even if one is aware of this, the music that often accompanies such words and videos is actually attractive and entrancing to the listener, which provides a channel for the meaning to be embodied, whether negative or positive.

The danger with negative meanings in music is that music reaches deep into our beings and can influence us in powerful and holistic ways. Just like food gives our bodies the energy they need to function, the quality of food can make all the difference in world. Food that is alive, natural, pure, fresh, and full of energy creates health, strength, and vitality, whereas food that is dead, artificial or processed, impure, or full of chemicals or toxins leads to stress, dis-ease, illness, and eventually disease. The same is true of the quality of sound and music that we consume. Music that portrays negative messages, violence, materialism, and sexism as goals to pursue creates stress and a dis-eased state of mind, which subsequently expresses itself as illness behavior and eventually as mental dysfunction and disease.

On the other hand, music that expresses the nobility of the human condition and encourages purity of thought, healthy relationships, and orients the mind to that which is spiritual, joyful, healthful, and unifying, will create health, strength, vitality, and a sense that all things are possible. Food, music, meditation, and experiences in nature are the fuel for the engine of your being. The quality of food that you put into your Super Power System will determine how it functions and the flow and speed at which you achieve your goals. So, take special care to give yourself quality musical fuel that will support your beautiful journey in creating a life of higher consciousness, happiness, and health, and wealth.

Brain States and Vibration

There are myriad variations that exist within the six aspects of vibration, all of which can be intertwined and are deeply complex within the context of music. These relate to ancient traditions of musical healing that worked for people in those times and places, wherein culture-specific music-healing technologies have been developed over time. While the same practices might work for a person from a different cultural time and place, it is rare, and often people become misguided and disappointed when their goals remain unachieved. But this need not be so. The key is to understand the difference between principles and practices that are culture-dependent and those that are universal.

For example, some research has attempted to create healthy brain states through biological entrainment. This occurs through what is called binaural beats, which is the combination of two vibrations whose frequencies are very close to each other, which generate a special kind of vibration that sounds like a regular beat or pulse. The brain can discern the difference between the frequencies and incorporate that frequency into the brain state. So, for example, if there is a frequency of 220 Hz against 224 Hz, the brain will calculate the difference of 4 Hz and that will appear in the brain state. The principle of entrainment, like all the principles and practices you will learn here, is powerful, but all of them can lose their efficacy if they are not practiced holistically in ways that are meaningful to YOU. Consider how, if a frequency that encourages a peaceful brain state is incorporated into a piece of music, the effect could be totally lost if the music is not suited to the taste of the listener. In that instance, the person can even become frustrated if they don't achieve their intended outcome. This is where your engagement with the process in the following chapters is critical. You are a co-creator of your practice, an active participant, rather than a passive observer. You will engage the Five Factors of your being, which will guide you to the insights you need to achieve your goals in any and all dimensions of life.

A few words about specific brainwaves will be important here to understand their role in moving from imbalance to balance. Brainwaves are discussed in terms of their speed, or rate of vibration, which is the same as their frequency measured in hertz (Hz). The brainwaves typically discussed are delta, theta, alpha, and beta. The brain usually produces all of these frequencies simultaneously. Thus, there is a kind of brainwave mix that exists and changes with the daily cycle of wakefulness and sleep. Whichever brainwave is dominant, we call that a state. For example, if a person's theta waves are predominant, that person is said to be in a theta state, even though all brainwaves are present. Importantly, specific activities and practices encourage certain frequencies/brainwaves more than others and this is precisely where sound, music, and meditation come in to help you create a desired brain state. You won't stop there, however; this is only a small part of the process. You will see this brain state as part of the holistic state of your being that includes all Five Factors: Body, Mind, Spirit, Emotions, and Relationships. Remember that, although such vibrations are physical and measurable frequencies, they are expressive of emotional and spiritual meanings and diverse bodily states.

Delta state brainwave frequencies or vibrations fall between 0.5 and 4 Hz (cycles per second) and most often occur in deep sleep. This state is also accessed through deep meditation and is associated with the unconscious, transcendent, or super-conscious mind, or the absence of the ego. This is often described as the letting go of the lower self through unconditional love or immersion in a spiritual realm. It is also associated with a healing potential and generative state of consciousness.

Theta state brainwaves span from 4 to 7 Hz. Theta state is associated with deep relaxation and meditation, a movement toward sleep, dreaming, creativity and insight, altered states of consciousness, and transcendence.

Alpha state brainwaves range from 7 to 12 Hz. Alpha state is associated with daydreaming, peace, relaxation, a greater wakefulness than theta, but with a sense of inward focus and calm.

Beta state brainwaves extend from 13 to 40 Hz. Beta state is associated with the active mind, daily tasks, and wakefulness. Higher levels of beta can also relate to stress and anxiety.

Good Vibes in Your Being

Brainwaves are only part of the process. If we return to the principle that all things are in vibration, we can consider vibrations or waves in all the Five Factors and all parts of our being. Accordingly, you can reflect on your emotional states of vibrations, or heartwaves, that will intuitively indicate to you your emotional state at different times and places. The notion of good vibes or bad vibes associated with certain people or places indicates to you the socialwaves that are palpable in any given situation. Your body is constantly sending you clear messages as to its state of vibration, being in tune or out of tune—whether it feels tight or loose, rigid or flexible, weak or powerful. These are bodywaves, or biowaves, that are fully integrated with your mind, heart, social self, and soul. Additionally, each cell, tissue, organ, and organ system has an optimal and healthy state of vibration. Finally, your soul expresses itself through vibrations or waves in all aspects of your being. It is the vital force of your life, an eternal transcendent energy that is delicately, powerfully, and mysteriously expressed though your body, being, and life. Any lack, illness, dysfunction, or problem can be seen as a barrier to the power of your soul and its full integration of your being. The final chapters work together, with you, step by step, to set out a practice that will enable you remove any barriers you might have and enter a state of being from which all things are possible.

A key to this process is the power of sound to carry meaning. Here, I focus on one very precious and special sound that only you possess. This is a sound that is unique throughout the history of the universe and all of humanity. This is the sound of YOUR voice.

Your Beautiful, Creative, Healing Voice

Yes, your voice is beautiful, and it possesses the power to heal you and create your new life. This might seem difficult to believe in the current popular culture that is totally opposite of what I am speaking of here. I am not talking about singing on a stage or in a music video. In fact, I am not even talking about singing in the conventional sense. Rather, I am speaking about the sounding of your inner being, your soul, which is expressed through your voice.

The voice has a great power for many reasons, a few of which are essential to the process of manifesting your new life. First, the word "manifest" means to create anew or bring into reality something that was hidden. Your voice is similar. Before you make any sound with your voice, it is fully within you, hidden as potential or unmanifest. Once you intone or sound your voice, it becomes active or manifest.

Of paramount importance here is that sound and music create the meaning they embody. In other words, sound is a vehicle of meaning that communicates and creates meaning throughout your being, so whatever meaning YOU give to your voice, that same meaning will be increased in ALL FIVE FACTORS of YOUR BEING and LIFE. Any thought (or meaning) that you have will be picked up by your Super Power System, and the more you focus on that thought, the faster you will move toward its manifestation in your life. Using sound, music, or your voice can increase the effectiveness of your meditation and speed along the process of manifestation.

In the following chapters, you will go through a step-by-step process to reflect and choose the reality that you will manifest in each of the Five Factors of your being and all of life. What you choose will form part of the content of your meditations that is specific to YOU. At that point, you can use your voice to create and manifest the focus of your meditations.

We will begin with the universal sound of Ahh. The sound Ahh is the most natural sound we can make. It is beautiful and immediately relaxes you, reduces stress, and invigorates your body and being. Just think about it. If you open your mouth when it is totally relaxed to make a sound without making any specific shape, the sound that emerges is Ahh! Also, Ahh is powerful is because it is a primal creative sound, and brings state of deep relaxation and peace. From this state of deep relaxation and peace, your recognition of your creative ability increases and you see the path unfold before you. So, repeating the sound Ahh with attention and intention to fully reflect the focus of your meditation will bring that reality into being.

Ahh is a creative sound, and whatever you have in your conscious attention can be linked to the creative power of this sound. Remember, before intoning the sound, it is unmanifest; it is potential that lies within you. As you allow the air and energy to rise up from within you, flow over your vocal chords, and make the sound Ahh, you will simultaneously link the sound to exactly what you desire to create in your life. This is an expression of the creative power of your soul, which, by definition, is always potential, and only partially manifest. By priming the power of the soul with sound, you tap into an infinite reservoir of energy that will naturally bring forth the intention you link to the sound —transforming the unmanifest into the manifest.

Ahh is also the beginning and the first sound of the ancient mantra Aum (or Om), which refers to the sound of the universe, the sound from which all creation arises and the inner sound of our beings. The last sound of Aum is the "mmm" sound when the lips come together; in between is the sound of the "O." So, the sound Aum is made by these three sounds "Ahh-O-mmm." In the traditions of yoga, these sounds are known as nada (Sanskrit for "sound").

Equally important is the silence that exists between each time you intone the sound Ahh or Om. In this silence, there is also sound, which in Sanskrit is known as anahata, or the unstruck sound, the sound that is ever-present, without beginning or end. There are many other simple yet powerful sounds and mantras that you can use in meditation and I'll be writing about these and giving examples in other books, blogs, articles, and recordings. For now, the Ahh and Om sounds are all you need to create the life you desire.

CHAPTER 8

Practical Steps for Transformation

"But, how can I get there from here?" she asked.
A voice replied, "One step at a time."
~

Beyond the GAP

GAP has two meanings here. First, it is an acronym for "Guided Attention Practice," a clear and powerful method of meditation that you will learn here and that you can use to recreate your life. I will serve as your partner in the process, walking with you, step by step, sharing ideas and practical techniques that will enable you to create that state of being through which all things are possible. As you practice the GAP method, you might use it exactly as I teach you here or you might modify it, creating your own personal practice of empowerment and transformation. You might also use the principles from GAP to apply to another meditation practice. All of these approaches are fine; whichever works best for you. Second, GAP refers to the space between your innermost heart's desire and its full expression in your life. Your innermost heart's desire is reflected by the inside-meditation list from chapter 5—in brief, it is only good and beautiful. Through the Guided Attention Practice, you will learn how to bridge the gap between the wondrous potential of your inner being and its manifestation in the fullness of your life. To get the full benefit of the meditation practice, you must first REFLECT on the Five Factors of your being. After the reflection process, you will then DECIDE and choose the most important thing you wish to integrate into your being through meditation. The final steps will be to PREPARE your body, MEDITATE, and ACT with purpose—to live your life as an extension of your meditation.

The Guided Attention Practice is a simple, straightforward, and effective way to create profound and beautiful changes in your life or to completely transform it. Over the years, as I shared my experiences of music and meditation with students and clients, it became clear that an open-ended framework for people to work with in meditation would be helpful and empowering for them. So, I created the GAP model. I also developed this approach of meditation as a way to clear up confusion for people who thought that meditation had to be complicated, religious, or take years to master. As you know now, those beliefs about meditation are primarily what make it difficult for so many people. They simply have the wrong idea to begin with. I have found meditation to be a bridge to health and healing, higher consciousness, and happiness. I created the GAP model to make meditation accessible to more people, to facilitate the unfolding and flourishing of a precious and wonderful life.

One of the most important ways to learn about meditation as well as how to meditate is through experiential learning, in other words, by doing and experiencing it. Even more important than this is the attitude you have about learning itself. True learning is both humbling and empowering. True learning also values what are often called "mistakes," since experiencing mistakes is absolutely necessary in order for learning to occur. I highlight this here so that, as you begin to experience and practice meditation, you will be encouraged with each step you take, and rather than viewing your learnings negatively as mistakes or problems, they will instead serve as helpful guides along your journey and positive indicators of your development. Each lesson that comes to you will be a gift, which, rather than being viewed as a stumbling block, will be a steppingstone along your path to fulfillment.

As you also know now, meditation is a natural part of life, essential nourishment for your being and a way to know your true self, which has limitless potential. You also recognize that meditation can enable you to fully manifest the life you desire, and that music, sound, and your own voice can be ladders of transformation. Before going through the 5 Steps process of REFLECT—DECIDE—PREPARE—MEDITATE—ACT, a brief description of the GAP approach is necessary.

Guided Attention Practice

The GAP process will work for you because it is driven by principles of spiritual truth, rather than strict rules and guidelines regarding the nonessential aspects of meditation. Equally important and exciting is that you will be a co-creator of your meditation practice. At its heart, this GAP approach of meditation will enable you to create the life you desire in all the Five Factors of your being, to achieve life and self-mastery, experience transcendence, and live a joyful, spiritual, healthy, and rich life.

As you learn different ways of meditation through the GAP process, you will begin to experience meditation as a dynamic journey along a spectrum of both mind states and states of being that you can induce, change, and direct. Your GAP process will serve as an initial framework within which you gain invaluable experience in meditation. Remember, meditation is both a process and a state of being. It is a process that moves from lower states of consciousness to higher states, and it is a state of being that bridges the gap between your daily awareness and your soul, ultimately integrating and unifying your being as an expression of all the potentialities of your spiritual reality. Key to this process is the knowledge that meditation does not end with each meditation session in the morning and evening. Rather, the meditation practice given here teaches you how to extend that blissful state of the meditative mind into your daily life.

Five Stages of the GAP

Stage 1:

Engage your body and mind to change your present state and prepare for Stage 2.

Stage 2:

Enter the state of your meditative mind.

Stage 3:

Embody a special word, idea, phrase, emotion, or goal into your meditative mind.

Stage 4:

Enjoy and experience the beauty, power, and bliss of your higher consciousness and soul. Feel your new reality as being fully present and true, NOW.

Stage 5:

Extend Stage 4 into your life activity (live life in your new reality).

The first time you practice your meditation, it's a lot like taking a walk to a new place for the first time, when you don't know the exact directions. The second time you meditate, the pathway and the destination is a little bit more familiar to you; the third time a bit more, and so on. With each meditation, the way becomes clearer and the destination deeper within you and easier to carry with you as you move your meditation session into the remainder of your day.

As you meditate each morning and evening, the empowering experience of the practice imbues both your waking and sleeping hours with a new energy. Then will you see, know, and experience that you are soul and have the power to heal yourself and your life, create happiness, and live in your higher spiritual consciousness at all times and under all conditions. We will return to the GAP model after you complete the first two steps of the Five-Step Reflect—Decide—Prepare—Meditate—Act process.

BEFORE YOU BEGIN, it is important to do this process at a time and place that is conducive to reflection. Choose a time and place where you will remain undisturbed for at least 30 minutes so you can focus on the reflection process. Once you have found a time and place, start with the action of "Turning Toward," which is an essential precursor to any process of transformation.

Turning Toward

Turning Toward means placing yourself in a state of humility, preparing yourself for reflection, and turning your whole being toward that which is the source of all things.

This can take infinitely diverse forms, perhaps as a form of prayer or meditation that you might already practice, or expressing it as opening your heart in silence with the intention of receiving.

However you choose to conceptualize "Turning Toward," you might just simply sit quietly, breath naturally and deeply, relax, and realize that you are beginning a powerful and transformative process. Breathe and be thankful for this opportunity. Continue to breathe naturally, allow your eyes to gently close, and exist in a state of deep relaxation for a moment. Once you feel that you have reached a state of humility and truthfulness, immediately move to Step 1. NOTE: If, at any time during the process you feel off track or interrupted from that place of humility and truthfulness, just take a few deep breaths, feel a sense of deep relaxation permeate your body, and remind yourself of that feeling you have now. OK, here we go.

Let's begin!

CHAPTER 9

Step One – Reflection & Step Two – Decide and Choose

Reflection:

By three methods we may learn wisdom: First, by reflection, which is noblest…
–Confucius

Without reflection, we go blindly on our way, creating more unintended consequences, and failing to achieve anything useful.
–Margaret J. Wheatley

Reflection draws on your life experience and higher consciousness to show you which path to take.
~

Decide & Choose:

Only you can control your future.
–Dr. Seuss

Every man got a right to decide his own destiny.
–Bob Marley

A real decision is measured by the fact that you've taken a new action.
If there's no action, you haven't truly decided.
–Tony Robbins

The Choice is Yours—Choose it, Be it, Live it, Now…

~

Positive power is key to success in my meditation program. Equally important is bringing your mind to the present moment of experiencing what you desire. Let me explain. First, you might have wanted or wished for something in the past but it never happens. You might even expect something to happen, and maybe it does, but maybe it doesn't. Why? Here I will explain a key to this mystery and then guide you through a simple exercise so you can experience it for your self.

The first key is to make sure you make this thing in a positive linguistic form. So, for instance, if you are ill and you chose that you want to be healthy, don't say this: "I don't want to be ill anymore" because that puts "be ill" in your brain and your mind will lead you towards creating more of being "ill". Instead, put it in the positive form. "I want to be healthy" is better, but still not good enough because it has a weak energy when compared with the best statement: "I am healthy", "I am health" or "I am well." Or for example, you can say "I am healthy, happy, whole and powerful." You can even add the power of gratitude and thankfulness to your phrase saying: "I am so thankful that I am healthy and strong." This is how you should form your core intention about what you want to be or create in your life.

Here is another example. If you have no money, don't choose the goal of: "I want to get out of debt" or "I want to make more money". Instead, use these or your own words to say "I am wealthy", "I am financially wealthy" or "I'm so happy and thankful to be wealthy" or "I am so grateful to have 5 million dollars in my bank account". Whatever it is, put it in the positive form of language and put it in the present tense: "I am so thankful that I am…" or "I am so grateful that I have…" This gives your brain the power it needs to create accurately what you focus on.

Remember that whatever is in your mind acts as a goal for your Super Power System. So, if you have anything negative in your mind about who you want to be or what you want to do, have, or create in your life, you must transform it into a POSITIVE POWER form. Let me give a real life example. A young woman we will call Linda went through this process in detail and found incredible benefit in the areas of health, happiness, self-confidence, courage, and finance. She agreed to share what she wrote so people could learn from her process. In Part A (which is the part you just finished), when she reflected on what she wanted to create and manifest in her being and life, here is what she wrote:

Summary of Linda's Reflection

1. I don't want to be stressed anymore; I'm always worried about something.
2. No depression.
3. I'm sick of being fat. I need to lose weight.
4. I want to be cured from my cancer.
5. I'm so tired all the time. I need energy.
6. I'm having conflict in my marriage and we have to resolve it.
7. I get angry or irritated and am so impatient—I want to change all this.

Considering these from the perspective of the Super Power System, ask yourself: What will be created as a result of these thoughts (or goals) being in Linda's mind? The answer is very telling and highlights the power of your Super Power System and the importance of casting your answers in the POSITIVE. Remember, your Super Power System simply sees thoughts as goals, without judgment, and will immediately move toward them. So, based on these excerpts, the following is exactly Linda would create if she were to keep these thoughts in her mind:

1. stress, worry
2. depression
3. sick, fat, weight
4. cancer
5. tired
6. conflict

7. angry, irritated, impatient

So, even though Linda wants to change these things, to move away from them, she would actually be creating more of the same problems because she has placed the problem, imbalance, or illness at the center of her attention and her Super Power System would faithfully lead her to what she has in her mind. This is why she needed to change her goals into a POSITIVE POWER form.

The list below illustrates how she transformed them into a positive form. In other words, POSITIVE LANGUAGE POWER creates the best of what you can BE and ARE in the fullness of your meditative mind, higher consciousness, or soul self. The reason is that language—each word, idea, and emotion—forms a COGNITIVE LINK in your mind, which becomes a steppingstone to the goal that the word, idea, or emotion represents. Consider the stark difference between the two types of language in the list below. Both are powerful, yet one perpetuates the ills and problems Linda does not want, while the other leads to a life she passionately desires and intends to create.

Negative: I don't want to be stressed anymore; I'm always worried about something.
Positive: I am peace, calm, relaxed, free.

Negative: No depression.
Positive: I am joy, enthusiasm.

Negative: I'm sick of being fat. I need to lose weight.
Positive: I am healthy, in control of my weight, balanced.

Negative: I want to be cured from my cancer.
Positive: I am pure, happy, love, healthy, whole.

Negative: I'm so tired all the time. I need energy.
Positive: I am energy, rested, vibrant, renewed.

Negative: I'm having conflict in my marriage and we have to resolve it.
Positive: I am patience, love, unity, selflessness.

Negative: I get angry or irritated and am so impatient—I want to change all this.
Positive: I am detached, accepting, patient, light-hearted, joyful, loving.

To highlight the place that meditation will play in the creation of your new reality, remember that the experience of BEING exactly what you decide and choose in your meditation is a REAL EXPERIENCE that you will have at the soul level or higher consciousness state of your meditation. This true experience will subsequently transfer into your daily life.

Consider then how important it is to see the truth of the POSITIVE realities you INTEND to create through your meditation. Now that you have recognized them, you no longer need to give any more attention to them—YOUR MIND, HEART, BODY, AND SOUL WILL NOW FOCUS ON THE POSITIVE.

Your attention is like water and sunlight for a plant. If you give your attention to the negative and dis-ease-causing thoughts, they will grow. On the other hand, if you give the food and energy of your attention to the positive realities you choose to create, they will grow and develop, bear fruit, and recreate your life, while all the negative aspects will fade away forever since they no longer are receiving the energy of your attention.

Okay, now for the second key to positive power. Here I'd like to guide you through a simple exercise to show you in a few minutes the power of your mind. First I want you to think of something that you'd like to have, it could be something simple like ice cream or something else like a new job, a healthy beautiful body, more money, or an experience like meeting someone new. Just choose something that you want. Okay, got it? Once you have it in your mind, let's make sure it has the first part of positive power, so put it into a positive power language form like I described above. Then, once you have it in a positive form, continue on with the exercise.

I want you to close your eyes and experience the sensation of "wanting, wishing, or hoping" that you get it. Take about ten seconds and see what it feels like to "want" "wish" or "hope" that you will get it.

Now, I want you to do the same thing, but this time I want you to have in your mind that you "expect" to actually get it. So, close your eyes for about 10 seconds and experience the feeling of "expectation" that you will get it.

Now I want you to repeat the exercise again , but this time I want you to have the feeling that you "know" you will get it, you have a "knowing" or "certainty" without any doubt that it will happen. Go ahead and close your eyes and experience this state.

Here is the last level: I want you to repeat the exercise one last time. Only this time I want you to close your eyes, breathe naturally and then see in your mind that you already have it, that it is true and real right now—feel it in your body and believe fully that it is true. Breathe naturally and experience this state as though you already have exactly what you want, in reality and in your life and feel it in your heart and body. Stay in this state of 10-20 seconds.

How do you feel? Do you notice the difference between the states? Usually people are shocked at the difference and sometimes even take a long time to come out of the last part where you see and feel it as real and true. Everyone I have ever done this with always feels closer to the thing they chose, and I'm sure you do too, even if only a little. You probably feel like its more possible to achieve it, you feel like it is more real and not so far away, and you feel more energy and joy from experiencing as real in your mind, even just for 10-20 seconds. Now imagine if you focus the power of meditation on creating a new reality and creating the life that you desire or dream of. You can move that dream into reality with my five step system. Remember, when you choose something to manifest in your life, it should be in a positive form and in the present, in the now.

Reflecting and then deciding and choosing the most important thing to be, have, do, or create is the beginning to the life you desire. Doing this will clarify your present state and mark a new beginning for you in the creation of your new life!

Happiness, Health, Wealth, and Wholeness

Now that you know the importance of positive language and putting your desired most important thing in the present tense, it is time for YOU to DECIDE and CHOOSE exactly what you feel you have to manifest in your life.

Here is your key question:

What is the most important thing

I honestly and passionately desire in my life?

or put another way:

What must I be, do, or have now?

This question is for YOU—your heart, soul, body and mind, and is for YOU to answer in total honesty. This question is not about anyone else's opinion about what you need to do or should want to do or be in your life—not your boss, your teacher, parents, children, or anyone else. The question is for you, and only you. Read the question again, now, and see if you instinctively know what it is. If you do, if you have a spark of insight and you know the answer, go ahead and write it down on a piece of paper or keep it in your mind.

If you're not sure, that's okay. You can start by reflecting on each of the five factors: your body, mind, spirit, emotions, and relationships and see what comes to your heart and mind as the most important thing you must be, do or have in your life. Okay, once you have it, write it down and make it into a positive language form like I showed you above.

Now I'm going to take you through a clarifying exercise below if you made a choice already or not. The exercise will help you to make a choice, or help you to make sure that you made the right choice.

The key is to choose the thing that you feel is right in your heart and in your body. Why is this important? Because when you choose the right thing, the thing that is truly the most important for you and that you truly and passionately desire, there will be alignment at all levels of your being and there will be a flow of energy toward creating that very thing that you choose.

How will you know if you choose the right thing? Well, first of all, if you instinctively know that its right, then trust it. If on the other hand you are not sure, then there are some signs you can pay attention to. First, when you touch on an answer you feel is it, you should feel excited in your heart and body, maybe even get some tingling sensation on your skin or butterflies in your belly. Second, take a deep breath and relax and consider what you have chosen. As you think about it, does a little smile come to your heart or face? Do you feel a little happier? Do you feel relieved, like you are being true to yourself or like a burden has been lifted from your shoulders? Do you feel like the thing you chose is exactly what you want but its just impossible or too difficult? Well, if any of these are true, you've probably chosen well!

So, if you haven't answered the questions yet, I will guide you through a brief breathing-meditation exercise for you to find an answer. First, I want you to breathe in for a count of four and breathe out for a count of four. Breathe in through your nose and out through your mouth. Let your breath be natural and unforced. With each breath, feel yourself relaxing more and more, feeling more peace and calm, more gratitude and forgiveness in your heart. Feel your mind open and your body relax, from the top of your head to the bottom of your feet, all over. Here we go:

Breathe in (relax)...1...2...3...4...and
breathe out (relax more)...1...2...3...4...

Do this three more times:
Breathe in (peace)...1...2...3...4...
breathe out (peace)...1...2...3...4...

Breathe in (forgiveness)...1...2...3...4...
breathe out (forgiveness) ...1...2...3...4...

Breathe in (gratitude)...1...2...3...4...
breathe out (gratitude)...1...2...3...4...

Now ask yourself the question again:

What is the most important thing
I honestly and passionately desire in my life?
What must I be, do, or have now?

When you come to an answer, feel it in your heart and body and see if you have a knowing that its right. If you still aren't sure, repeat the breathing exercise above but this time put one or both hands on your heart or your heart chakra in the middle of your chest, or put one hand on your heart and the other hand on energy center called your dan tian in Chinese medicine and philosophy, which is just below your navel. Do the breathing exercise again and allow your truth to come to your heart and mind.

Once you have it, make sure its in a positive power form of language like we did above and write it down or remember it. Now I want you to see what you have chosen in your mind, envision it as though it is real and say it out loud to yourself. Breathe naturally and relax and keep this feeling in your mind and body alive.

Congratulations—Well Done!

You have reached a point that few people ever do. If this is the first time that you have thought deeply about exactly want you must create in your life and then decided what you want to create and manifest in them, take a deep breath and feel a sense of loving gratitude and joyful energy emerging in your being—you are one step closer to all that you have identified for your new and wonderful life. If you have considered such things before, but have not yet seen them created and manifested in your life, breathe deeply and feel a renewed sense of thankfulness and heightened energy of joy, momentum, and certainty, because, in the next steps, you will finally discover and feel that power to create and transform what is within you. If you have already discovered this power and have had success in using it, take a deep breath of gratitude and know that your next steps will propel you beyond your present experience and give you a sense of bliss and power that you may have yet only faintly imagined.

We will now move to the next step.

CHAPTER 10

Steps 3 & 4
~Prepare &
Meditate

Your mind, body, and spirit are strengthened during meditation.
The unknown becomes known and you open the door to your new reality.

~

Action is the foundational key to all success.
–Pablo Picasso

The success of meditation is manifest through your action.

~

Mind into Matter and Beyond

In this chapter, you will begin your meditation. As you practice consistently, every morning and evening, and as you allow the focus of your soul to enter that dynamic and creative space of your meditative mind, you will notice your life beginning to change. You will experience the bliss of living in the moment as you learn from your soul-self how to be here now. You will notice a greater connection with nature and all living things, you will witness how your life progressively aligns itself with the content of your meditations, and you will move from a lower vibration of energy to a higher vibration that is transformative, lighthearted, joyful, and loving. In ways that you might not yet see, you will grow in the areas of happiness, health, and wealth.

Below, you will begin your meditations with the focus that you decided on and wrote in the box at the bottom of STEP 2, Part C, in the last chapter. This process will focus on one technique and approach that is simple yet profound, one that is deeply fulfilling and empowering, which will enable you to create your new reality. Here we go!

Step 3 ~ Prepare

First, retrieve the sheet of paper marked "Part C" from the last chapter where you wrote your empowered words or phrase that express the Core Power and Essence of what you will create and manifest in your WHOLE BEING and LIFE.

Loosen or remove any tight or uncomfortable clothing or jewelry. Find a comfortable place to sit, stand, or lie down for your meditation.

Stretch Your Body and Prepare Your Mind

Here you can perform any stretches to loosen your body and become more flexible and relaxed. Stretching your body, even a little bit, activates the cognitive link in your mind and heart to become flexible and ready to create change in life. If you are not familiar with how to stretch your body, I suggest the following simple yet powerful movements, which you can perform seated or standing. This is also a simple and effective approach for you if you are highly experienced with stretching. Breathe, relax, and let your hands rest in a natural position at your side, if standing, or on your thighs, if seated, and do the following:

Gently Nod and Turn Your Head

To relax your neck and upper shoulders, gently nod your head, taking about four seconds to go down and four more seconds to return to the original position. Then, taking the same amount of time, gently turn your head to the left, and then back to the center, then to the right, and then back to the center. Do this a few times.

Make Big Circles with Your Arms—Opening and Closing/Gathering Circles

This stretch has many powerful benefits: in your body, it opens your chest, upper body, shoulders, and internal organs. In your body's energy system, the opening circle opens your heart chakra (your emotional center), connects your crown chakra to the source of life, and vitalizes all your chakra energy centers. With the closing/gathering circle, you are gathering energy from the universe and internalizing it, inviting it to flow from the top of your head, throughout your chakras and your body, all the way to your feet, strongly rooting them into the earth's energy.

Opening Circles

As you perform this stretch, you will inhale as your raise your arms all the way up above your head, and then exhale as you lower them to their original position, all in one continuous fluid motion.

Start with your arms at your side. Begin to raise your arms forward, with your palms facing each other. Your arms extend directly in front of you (parallel to the ground and perpendicular to your body)—no need to pause, just keep the motion going upward until your arms are extending straight into the sky, like you are a long, extended bamboo, palms still facing each other. Now begin to exhale and let your palms turn out and away from each other, which will naturally direct your arms to descend on the sides of your body. Continue to exhale as you lower your arms, your palms progressively and naturally turned towards the ground and coming back into their original position, all in one continuous fluid motion.

This stretch can also be performed the following way: in the beginning, instead of raising your hands directly in front of you, bring your hands together, palms touching each other, in front of your chest, in a prayer-like position. Keeping your palms together, inhale and gently raise your arms until they are fully extended straight above your head with your palms still touching. Then, at the top position, open your hands, turning your palms outward and, slowly exhaling, let your arms float down all the way to their original position at your side. Do this movement of the opening circles at least three times.

Closing/Gathering Circles

As you perform this stretch, you will inhale as your raise your arms all the way up above your head and exhale as they return to the original position. Starting with your hands at your side, gently extend and raise your arms to your sides (not in front of you this time) and let your palms turn upward as your arms rise. Raise your hands all the way above your head until your palms are facing each other but not touching. Then, as you slowly bring your arms down, turn your palms face down, with your fingertips almost touching. Your hands will descend in front of your face, followed by the chest and belly. Then, simply let your arms return to their original position. Do this movement of the closing/gathering circles at least three times.

You can do these simple stretches alone or in combination with others that work for you.

Meditation for a Happy, Healthy, Wealthy YOU!

NOTE: Below I will guide you through two meditations, one longer, and the other shorter. Read through both sections and follow the process as best you can to get a feel for it first, before attempting it. At the end of this chapter, I summarize the shortest version of the meditation in three stages so you can remember it easily—this is what is important. You don't need to do it exactly as I guide you below—the most important aspects that will bring you success are summarized at the end. However, for many people, the details noted in the longer version immediately below are important to bring powerful and lasting changes. You can refer to the summary or to this whole section to remember the process and develop your own personal approach.

Here we go!

1. After stretching and preparing your body and mind, breathe deeply and naturally a few times, relax, and let a feeling of thankfulness come into your heart. Breathe and feel gratitude spread throughout your body and being. Allow your attention to move to your lungs and breathe— feel your lungs expand as they fill with oxygen. With each breath, your body relaxes and your energy flows more freely. Now, let your attention move to your shoulders, upper back, and neck. Breathe as though you are breathing

with these parts of your body—breathe into them and exhale through them.

Breathe with your belly, chest, back, shoulders, and neck altogether...relax and feel your body relax and your energy gently increase. Now, we will move your mind slowly throughout your body—feel your belly relax and open, and then your lower back, waist, pelvic area, thighs, knees, calves, shins, ankles, heels, feet, and toes. Slowly bring your mind back to your lungs. Breathe thankfulness, purity, and energy into your lungs and feel it in your chest...now moving to your shoulders, your spine and back muscles, your arms, hands, neck, face, forehead, and ears, and up the back of your head, across the top and all throughout your head.

Breathe with your WHOLE BODY several times. Now, in this more relaxed and flexible state, read what you wrote in response to the question:

What is my passionate desire and core intention to create and manifest in my whole BEING and LIFE?

Read your answer out loud few times, and then repeat it silently in your mind, breathing in and out deeply and naturally, feeling in your body the power and meaning of the words you are reading, and then continue the steps as outlined below.

2. Allow this focus to be in the front of your mind and let that word or phrase rest in that open space of your consciousness. Gently close your eyes and feel what you have written in your body and see yourself as having

attained the state you desire. If you want to be at a different weight, see yourself in your mind's eye at your new weight. If you have chosen vitality and energy, envision yourself as vibrant and full of energy. If there is part of your body that you want to heal, see that part healed and healthy—see your whole body and being in total health. Whatever you have chosen to focus on, let that come to your mind and breathe it, feel it, see it, know it as being fulfilled, a reality—then take a natural and full breath and make a long vocal sound on the word Ahh or Om. Make the sound wherever it feels comfortable in your voice. As you repeat the sound a few times, let your voice relax and the pitch become lower—the lower sound will relax you and resonate deeper in your body, in the areas of your lower chakras. As sound is a vehicle of meaning, let the Ahh or Om sound, which emerges from deep within you, carry the meaning of your meditation from inside your being to a full and real expression in your life—feel the strength, health, healing, peace, energy, vitality, and certitude; feel the knowing that you are transforming to embody the attributes, qualities, and reality that you have chosen. Breathe and repeat the sound while focusing on the specific word, words, phrase, or idea you have chosen as the core intention that you will manifest in all your being and life.

3. Continue this for a few minutes, letting your voice unfold naturally, allowing any sound to emerge as it will, moving lower or higher in pitch as it feels best. See the sound carry the meaning of your meditation throughout your

body and being.

NOTE: If there is a place in your body that you are focusing on for healing or any kind of change, you can place one or both hands on that area. Or, if you are focusing on a total body healing, wellness, or transformation, you can place one or both hands wherever you intuitively feel they should go. A few options of strong positioning for your hands is to place both in the middle of your chest on your heart chakra; both hands just below or on your navel area; or one hand in each of these places. You can also move one hand to your forehead while keeping the other hand on your chest or navel area. Keep an open mind and experiment with these positions.

4. Restate the focus of your meditation and now see yourself (your body, mind, spirit, emotions, relationships, and wealth) in your mind as being exactly what you desire. Strengthen the sound of Ahh or Om, bringing more power into your voice, with complete acceptance and knowing that this is YOU, and make the sound Ahh or Om. Do this for a few more minutes.

NOTE: You can experiment with the following or move directly to number 5. The following can be a particularly powerful technique to add to your Ahh sound: as you make the sound, envision the sound as a warm and bright white light, emerging from within you and slowly filling the space around you, growing with each Ahh (or Om) sound, continuing to expand until it fills the room you are in (if you feel the light should be particular color, you can experiment with that as well. Colors correspond to different frequencies and chakras and can be aligned with your particular needs and intentions). As you continue to make the creative sound, full of your new reality, see the sound and light flow outside of the room to fill the house or building you are in. Continue expanding the sound-light with each repetition of Ahh or Om, until the sound-light fills the space outside of your home, expanding to your city, and then the state, province, or region, your country and continent, expanding across the planet into space, filling the universe. Feel the sound-light vibration filling the universe with your manifest desire. Allow your mind to move beyond any and all words, all ideas, concepts, everything, (even letting go of the focus of your meditation). Allow your mind, your body, and your being to be totally free, and make the sound Ahh or Om for as long as you like.

5. When you feel it is time, let the sound of your voice rest in silence and allow yourself to simply be in the sacred space of your higher consciousness now, without sound, without a specific focused thought—fully open and at one in soul. Be here, now, in this state as long as you like, breathing naturally and gently.

6. When you decide, start to bring your attention back to the front of your consciousness, continuing to breathe deeply and naturally.

NOTE: If you used the technique of expanding your consciousness with the sound and light, you can now slowly return the light from the expanse of the universe to yourself, moving step by step until the sound-light is returned to your body, heart, and mind. You can use the sound Ahh, Om, or, with your lips together, you can hum, making a gentle mmm sound. Slowly move the sound-light back to your heart and throughout your body and being.

7. Stay in this state of peace and contemplation for a few minutes. As you stay in this open state, special thoughts, ideas, and feelings will come to you. Some of the thoughts and ideas will not require any action; they will simply be passing waves of energy. Some thoughts will be healing energy that you will feel throughout your body or in particular places in your body and being. These are sacred thoughts and energy—rest in this energy and experience the vitality and healing power. Some thoughts or ideas will relate to actions you must take as they specifically relate to your new reality, to creating the life you have envisioned and experienced in your meditation. When such a thought or idea comes, this is one to remember and write down afterward.

As you practice your meditation, if you choose, you can pause to write something down (place a pad and pen next to you before you start meditating, if you would like to do this; we'll talk more about this in chapter 12), then close your eyes again and continue that state of insight when more thoughts will come for you to take action on. You can also choose not to pause and write anything down but, rather, remember it or simply let it go and it will return in its own time after meditation or in a subsequent meditation. It's also totally fine if nothing comes to mind —just experience the bliss of this state at the end of your meditation. You are about to arise and take action in your new reality.

8. Now as you fully come back to your conscious awareness, you will notice that your feelings, your thoughts, your body, and even your field of vision are fresh and new, more vibrant, empowered, and directed. This is because you have just experienced the reality of your new life in your meditation. Now, immediately take action in your new reality as you are directed by your inner sense of knowing. If you wrote something down during your meditation, immediately take action toward accomplishing that—you might be able to do it on your own, or you might need to enlist the expertise of a friend, colleague, or professional in the area you are working on.

If you did not write anything down, then immediately arise and begin your day in your new reality. Be aware that you are extending that feeling from meditation throughout your daily activities. Let that state of meditation frame your experience throughout the day. If you feel it slipping away, all you have to do is recall the focus of your meditation in the moment. Specifically, recall the word, words, phrase, or feeling that was the focus of your meditation. This is your cognitive link to the highpoint and power of your meditation. If you can, close your eyes, take a deep breath, and recall the focus of your meditation. You will immediately re-experience a degree of the highpoint of your meditation and gain the necessary power you need in the moment. You can also add a gentle Ahh or Om sound to your meditative moment! This will supercharge the experience and bring even a greater degree of power to the moment. Now, ride the wave of your meditation and live your new life to the fullest!

Summary Steps for Meditation

1. Prepare for meditation by taking a few deep and relaxing breaths. Do any gentle stretches or movements to prepare your body and mind to enter the state of meditation. Read aloud the focus of your meditation and repeat it in your mind silently. Breathe with your whole body and feel the focus of your meditation in your body.

2. Gently close your eyes and feel in your body that which is the focus of your meditation and see yourself as having attained the reality you desire. Take a natural and full breath and make a long vocal sound on the word Ahh or Om. Let the sound carry the meaning of your meditation and make it stronger and stronger. Continue this and see the focus of your meditation growing within you. Then, see the focus of your meditation extend outside of you and be fully manifest in your life. See in your mind what you have chosen as being fulfilled and know that it is real. Feel

this reality and experience this state as long as you like (from a few moments to 30 minutes). If you like, you can use any hand placements on your body or visualizations to strengthen the power of your meditation.

3. Finally, gently open your eyes and continue breathing in the same way as during your meditation. Keep the focus and feeling of your meditation fully present, with your eyes now open. As you arise from your meditation, extend the feeling of your new reality into every action, every step, every breath, and everything you do throughout the day. Repeat your meditation at night before you sleep. Live your life to the fullest!

CHAPTER 11

Step 5 ~ Act with Purpose

And as you act, you, yourself, will become a magnet,
which will attract more power to your being,
until you become an unobstructed channel for the
divine power to flow through you.
–Attributed to Shoghi Effendi

Little by little, day by day.
–'Abdu'l-Bahá

Stumbling Blocks to Steppingstones

Anything that lies in your path can either be a stumbling block or a steppingstone—it all depends on you and how you choose to view it. When you arise from your morning meditation with a mindset of purposeful action, each step takes you closer to a fuller expression of the reality that you experienced in your meditation. After your morning meditation, you will arise and extend the state of meditation into everything you do. At first, be very mindful of every aspect of your experience and make it a conscious expression of the focus of your meditation.

Here is an example:

Let's say that the focus of your meditation was to redesign your body, achieve your ideal weight (which meant you needed to lose 20 pounds), become fit and firm, gain energy and vitality; and that you chose this phrase as the focus of your meditation:

I am strong, healthy, pure, and fit.

Now, imagine that after your morning meditation, you truly felt this sense of being strong, healthy, pure, and fit in your body and your entire being. So, after meditation, perhaps you had a tall glass of water with fresh lemon juice and enjoyed a healthy breakfast of fruits, nuts, and a bowl of all-natural muesli with coconut milk. You feel great, and like you've accomplished a great step toward your goal of redesigning your body. Now, imagine that you go to work, have a cup of coffee (this is good!) and generally feel connected to your meditation, until about 11:00am. Perhaps you're getting a bit sluggish, hungry, maybe encountered some conflicts with clients or co-workers, and by the time lunch comes around, you've forgotten about the focus of your meditation and you are now at the local restaurant ready to order your lunch and are looking at a host of poor nutritional choices.

Just as you are asked what you'd like to order, a little voice inside reminds you how great you felt after meditation and your healthy breakfast. So, you tell the waiter that you need another minute. You sit at the table and decide to recall the focus of your meditation. This alone is a great victory! Sitting at your table, you close your eyes, take one deep breath and immediately your recall the focus of your meditation—in the twinkling of an eye, the words that you chose flash to the front of your mind:

I am strong, healthy, pure and fit.

You breathe again and instead of making the Ahh sound strong and loud, you gently hum the sound mmm. This immediately brings a deeper level of connection to your meditation and a smile appears on your face. You realize that there is almost nothing in that restaurant to both satisfy your hunger and keep you true to your new reality of being strong, healthy, pure, and fit. You consider ordering a baked potato and making a trip to the salad bar for some fresh veggies, sprinkled with sunflower and pumpkin seeds, olive oil, and balsamic vinegar, but you think you'll save that for another day. You feel like moving your body! So, you get up and walk out.

There is a grocery store next door. Now that you are moving your body and still thinking of the focus of your meditation, I am strong, healthy, pure, and fit, you are getting happier, stronger, and there is a spring in your step. You pop into the store, the bell jingles as the door opens, and you say a bright "Hello" to the young man at the cash register. You pick up a basket, take a quick stroll around, and get some hummus, Greek olives, cherry tomatoes, cucumbers, and carrot sticks. You find a bench to sit on outside and enjoy your lunch with a feeling of success and that you are in control of your life. You know you are not only one step closer to your body goals, but that you can and will achieve anything you set your mind to.

Building from this example, let's continue to say that being strong, healthy, pure, and fit is the focus of your meditation. So, "I am strong, healthy, pure, and fit" becomes the theme and reality that you will extend into all your daily experience as best you can. In other words, every action will be a conscious expression of strength, health, purity, and being fit.

As you prepare your breakfast, "I am strong, healthy, pure, and fit" will be the atmosphere within which you make and eat your breakfast. If there is something you notice in your refrigerator that is not strong, healthy, pure, and fit, immediately throw it away and congratulate yourself! As you get dressed for the day, "I am strong, healthy, pure, and fit" will frame your experience of getting dressed—if there are any clothes that are not in harmony with being strong, healthy, pure, and fit, immediately throw them out or donate them to charity, and congratulate yourself again!

Be aware of your breathing: your lungs taking in fresh air, expanding as you inhale, carrying the energy of your meditation into your body, and then expressing power as you exhale. Feel the ground or floor underneath your feet as you walk. If you make a cup of tea or coffee, be aware of the smells, the sound of the water boiling, and the feel of the cup in your hand. Realize that at every moment you are achieving more and more success in being strong, healthy, pure, and fit—you are living that reality.

Carry the reality of your meditation into all aspects and dimensions of your daily experience. If you have a meeting or appointment planned during the day, how will you prepare for it or think about it? Let the strength, health, and purity from your meditation pervade the quality of your meeting or appointment. Likewise, for any spontaneous interactions with other people throughout the day, be aware of your state —let your interactions flow in a pure and strong way; and remember that all the virtues are connected and express degrees of each other. So, for example, the virtue of strength might help you to be brave, courageous, or disciplined in one situation and gentle, flexible, and patient in another. All of these can be seen as expressions of strength and this can help you maintain an awareness of how your Super Power System can support you in diverse situations, which might call for different virtues and actions in different contexts.

Troubleshooting—Keep Moving Forward!

If you are walking on a tightrope, or trying to walk across a narrow bridge, there is a reason why they say, "Don't look down!" It is because, if you look down, you might fall. In other words, you might move in the exact direction your attention is focusing, even if it is somewhere that you don't want to go! Sound familiar? This is your Internal Super Power Success System in action. Remember that what you focus on, what you think, say, and do, creates more of what you are thinking, saying, and doing. If your thoughts are scattered, weak, or unclear, your results will be scattered, weak, and unclear; but if your thoughts are focused, strong, and clear, so will your results be. Stagnation results from one of two things. Either a person is having stagnant thoughts, which creates more stagnation; or the person is having a powerful and positive thought, followed by a weak and negative thought, or similar opposing thoughts one after the other, which basically results in taking one step forward followed by one step backward, or two steps forward and one step back, as it were—never really breaking new ground and feeling stuck in a rut.

The key to creating a full expression of the content of your meditation is to, first, be aware of your thoughts and actions and, second, increase daily the degree to which you extend the reality of your meditation into your daily activities. If you can only keep the reality that you experienced during your meditation present in your daily action for one minute, that's okay. Tomorrow, make it two minutes! If you continue to double your time every day, by the tenth day of meditation, you will be up to over eight hours of extending the reality of your meditation into your daily lived experience! That is not only incredible—it is doable!

To really do it, you must have a truly meaningful focus for your meditation—it must be something that makes your heart beat a little faster or stronger, gives you goose bumps on your skin, butterflies in your belly, or some other physical, emotional, or spiritual inspiration or state change. In other words, you should feel a rise when you think of it! It is like thinking of someone whom you love and the tangible emotional experience that comes along with that thought. The focus of your meditation must be something that is

MOST IMPORTANT to you and something that is an absolute MUST HAVE or MUST BE, not just a "nice to have" or "that would be good if..." kind of feeling.

The focus of your meditation should generate in you excitement, enthusiasm, a feeling of passion and energy, and increase your personal will to achieve it. If you are not getting the results you think you should be, the reason could be that your focus is not a MUST HAVE or MUST BE. In other words, what you have chosen to focus on in your meditation might simply lack the energy it needs to rally the forces of your Super Power System to reach higher levels of manifesting your desires. If that is the case, your experience will never reach beyond the mediocre "so-so" realm of existence. This is kind of like having a super-powered Maserati that only uses a few horsepower to drive in circles in places it's already been to and doesn't really like; or never venturing into the deep end of the pool or jumping off the high dive when that is exactly what you want to do, deep in your heart.

To manifest the reality of your meditation, remember that what you want to manifest must be the most important thing for you at this time in your life. So, first be sure that this is indeed the case. If you have chosen the most important thing, then great! Keep going! If you have not chosen a must-have or must-be as the focus of your meditation, then STOP right now and take a moment to have a quick and brutally honest conversation with your inner being. Take a few deep breaths and ask yourself:

What is the MOST IMPORTANT must-have or must-be for me right now at this time in my life?

When you have the answer, return to chapter 11 to do your meditation with a renewed sense of purpose and let your new focus guide your meditation.

As you keep both your external and internal vision directed toward the focus of your meditation, you will slowly and surely move in that direction until you achieve everything that you have imagined in your heart of hearts and experienced in your meditation. Then, you will realize other dreams and goals and be altogether living from a different place that is beautiful, powerful, and joyous.

Track Your Experience

I strongly recommend that you keep a journal of your experiences during at least the first month of meditation. For 30 days, I want you to write about three things:
1. Your experience during meditation.
2. Your experience during the day.
3. Your experience of sleep and your dreams.

If you already keep a journal or have in the past, this will be a very natural and fun process for you. If you have never kept a journal or are opposed to it, I recommend that you try it for 30 days. After 30 days, continue your meditation with or without the journal. Once you feel that that you have achieved your goals and decide to create a new focus, or if you decide to change the focus of your meditation before 30 days have passed, I strongly advise you to journal again with this new focus in mind. Your journal should be simple and easy to write. It can be a basic notepad, book, or a digital device, whatever works best for you. Let's take a look at what to do for your journal.

Morning Meditation

Set your journal beside you during your meditation. Immediately after your meditation, write freely, without censoring your thoughts or feelings. First, write down any action items, answers, or insights that came to you during meditation. Then, write about your experience during meditation. How did you feel? What was it like? Describe the state you entered in your meditative mind. Describe the process that you used for meditation. Was there anything special you did that was helpful or powerful? Any of these and other thoughts that you freely write will bring insight to you now or later as you reflect on your meditation over the coming days and weeks. You can write for as little or as long as you like. Let this information inform and improve your process. There will also likely be sensations and experiences during meditation that are beyond words—this is fine. Just feel them and remember them. They can form an important part of your progress.

Next, you will arise with your sense of meditation still intact and begin today in a new and empowered state. As you extend your meditation into your daily activities, pay close attention to everything that happens today. Things that might seem unimportant, or something that you might not have paid attention to previously, might actually be a key in manifesting your new life or attaining the goals that relate to the focus of your meditation.

There might also be very clear signs or experiences that are obviously a result of your meditation. When you have a moment, note these in your journal as well. In addition, write about your overall feeling during the day as it relates to the focus of your meditation. In what ways did you feel closer to the reality of your meditation? Were there any stumbling blocks and steppingstones throughout the day? How did you recall the focus of your meditation during such moments to help you turn the stumbling blocks into steppingstones? Be specific and express your gratitude and happiness for every victory or insight you had throughout the day. All that you write in your journal should be related to the focus of your meditation—this is what will inform your process for your subsequent meditation sessions.

You can write about your experiences during the day at any time that is most convenient. You can set aside a specific time during the day or keep your journal with you and jot down ongoing notes throughout the day as you have key experiences and inspirations. Your experiences might occur spontaneously and seemingly miraculously, or they might happen as a consequence of conscious systematic planning and action—both are important to journal about, as they will further empower you and give momentum to your life.

Keep in mind that the journal is a reflective tool that is a supplement to your meditation and serves as a kind of mirror for you to consider the process from a different perspective. It should not get in the way of your experience. So, if something happens during the day that you clearly see as being important, keep going with it, and don't stop to journal about it—you can do that later! And if you are worried that you'll forget about it if you don't write it down, that's okay too—if it is truly important for you to remember, you will, to be sure. Keep it light and enjoy the process!

Evening Meditation

Again, have your journal beside you. If you meditate just before sleeping, you might have some important insight that you want to write down before you sleep. This is fine. It is also fine to meditate and let yourself drift off to sleep. In either case, when you awake, be sure to journal about your meditation, your quality of sleep, and write about your dreams. If you don't remember your dreams, then before you sleep, tell yourself (i.e., let your soul tell your mind) to remember your dreams so that when you wake up, you will have the knowledge and experience from your dream state.

Additionally, you can tell yourself how to sleep and use your dreams for working out anything that you'd like to while sleeping. The dream state can be a kind of meditation also, wherein you can experience the focus of your meditation in its full expression, find answers to questions, or gain insight about anything that you focus on during your sleep.

Spiraling Upward

This process is like an upward spiral that carries you higher and higher into the reality that you have decided to create.

Let me outline it briefly. You are beginning a process of meditating both morning and evening, and then extending the meditative state into your daily activities, recalling your meditation throughout the day by linking your mind to the focus of your meditation, and even re-experiencing the highpoint of meditation whenever you desire throughout the day. Then you are adding the reflective experience of journaling. All this is truly a creative and transformative process that will imbue your every moment with a new power and fresh perspective.

Share Your Experience

I invite you to share your experiences with me directly by emailing me at ben@benkoen.com. In the subject line, write: "My Meditation Experience" so I'll be sure to get it. I would love to hear from you about how the 5 Steps have served you in creating the life you desire, experience healing or transformation, or help you reach your goals and dreams. In addition, I'd love to hear any questions or challenges you might have. In my experience, there has never been a situation that cannot be overcome, and this interaction can be key in the process. I have a section of my blog dedicated to this, so you can send these along as well and I'll get back to you through the blog or a personal email.

Remember SEA and the 5 Steps!

Whether you will use this material to embark on a new journey or to support a journey that you have already begun,

I call to your attention the three points of the SEA Meditation I briefly introduced at the beginning of the book, and the summary of the 5 Steps. Memorize these and keep them in the front of your mind along with the focus of your meditation.

SEA Meditation Outline

See, **E**xperience, **A**ct

1. *See* the end in the beginning.
   (See your end goal clearly at the beginning of any endeavor.)
2. *Experience* that end as real, now, in your meditation.
3. *Act* as though your goal has already been achieved.

These simple but powerful points have provided an invaluable path and process for people to achieve their goals and create the life they desire. Read them, memorize them, reflect upon them, and use them every day. Remember, this is at the heart of the 5 Steps to a Happy, Healthy, Wealthy You!

5 Steps Outline

I. REFLECT on the Five Factors of life (body, mind, spirit, emotions, relationships) and write down where you are now and what you passionately desire to create in each factor and in life as a whole.

2. DECIDE and choose the most important thing that you have written in Step 1—that which you must have or be.

3. PREPARE your body to meditate (this can take from a few seconds to a few minutes).

4. MEDITATE—Enter the state of meditation and see that which you have chosen as being fully real and true, now, in your meditation. Be that which you have chosen in your meditation. Feel the sensation in your body, heart, and soul that you are that reality.

5. ACT—Arise from your meditation and immediately take action in your new reality.

To a Happy, Healthy, Wealthy YOU!

CONGRATULATIONS! If you are ready to go to the next level to create the life of your dreams, if you are ready to breakthrough to the next level in any area of life, I invite you to sign up for a free one-hour Happy-Healthy-Wealthy Breakthrough Session with me or one of my trained team members. I have developed a special process where we will do a deep dive on your inner truth, passionate desire, and vision, then we will discover the path for you to create that reality. Sign up here: www.drben.acuityscheduling.com and see you soon!

About the Author

Benjamin D. Koen, Ph.D. has dedicated his life to bringing happiness, love, health, and true wealth to humanity. His mission· is to help you tap into your innate creative and generative powers and to live from that place of truth and freedom where you can experience health and vitality, and the manifestation and flourishing of your unique truth and life. Ben does this by living and teaching his fresh and deep understanding and practice of music, the mind, and meditation. Simple, yet profound, Ben's approach helps you to realize your inner truth and the real you. From there you learn how to extend the real you fully into your daily life to create and live what is true in your heart and inner being. you learn how to extend the real you fully into your daily life to create and live what is true in your heart and inner being. you learn how to extend the real you fully into your daily life to create and live what is true in your heart and inner being.

Email Ben here: ben@benkoen.com, or visit www.benkoen.com, or join the newsletter and Sound Health Global community here https://benkoen.activehosted.com/f/3Email

Notes

Notes

www.ingramcontent.com/pod-product-compliance
Lightning Source LLC
Chambersburg PA
CBHW060926040426
42445CB00011B/820